Advance Praise

"A big thank you to Kristine Cherek for writing *Tread Loudly*, which offers superb real-world advice for women starting their careers. Kristine is a wonderful storyteller. Rather than saying 'Take the risk!' she shows how it's done. *Tread Loudly* is wise, warm, full of insights, and a lot of fun to read. Highly recommended!"

—**Sally Helgesen**, author, *Rising Together*, *How Women Rise*, and *The Female Advantage*, premiere expert on leadership, and international speaker

"If you want real, practical advice for building a successful career in any business without sacrificing who you are and what makes you unique, this book is for you. In a compelling series of personal stories and pop-culture references, Kristine outlines the complicated dynamics that contribute to inequality in the workplace, how it leads to a lack of women in senior leadership, and calls on corporate America to finally make the changes necessary to improve the retention and promotion of women."

—**Elissa Sangster**, CEO, Forté Foundation, and expert on women in business leadership

"In *Tread Loudly*, author Kristine Cherek uses her own experiences in the legal field as the basis to give readers a down-to-earth pep talk about what they must do to achieve career success. Focusing on the many subtle (and some not-so-subtle) challenges in the workplace, she provides tips for how you can manage them with confidence and the knowledge that you are certainly not alone."

—**Lois P. Frankel, PhD**, author, *Nice Girls Don't Get the Corner Office* and *Nice Girls Don't Speak Up or Stand Out*, keynote speaker, and executive coach

"*Tread Loudly* is a candid account of Kristine Cherek's experiences in corporate America and her efforts to succeed personally and professionally. Both humorous and sobering, this book is a welcome and useful collection of career advice for upcoming generations of women entering the workplace."

—Veronica Vargas Stidvent, Executive Director, The Center for Women in Law, The University of Texas School of Law

"I love women who aren't afraid to stand up to the status quo and demand change for women. Kristine Cherek is exactly that kind of woman. Her book is the kind of thing young women need as a roadmap in navigating the male-dominated workforce."

—Brittany Butler, former CIA officer and author, *The Syndicate Spy*

"Kristine Cherek's book gives an authentic and beautifully messy view into the worklife for many women, encouraging them to embrace this messiness and not run from it. As an organizational psychologist studying women's untold stories at work, I found Kristine's book provided so many useful rallying cries for women as they carve out their ideal sense of self at work, and it's a valuable resource for men who are looking for ways to break down the barriers that continue to exist."

—Allison S. Gabriel, PhD, Thomas J. Howatt Chair in Management, Purdue University, Daniels School of Business

"Kristine Cherek's *Tread Loudly* shows that despite inroads, corporate America has a lot of work to do to address gender inequality. A must-read for professionals, this book shines a light on the headwinds women face in their careers and challenges readers to push out of their comfort zone to find the boldness within to claim their professional dreams."

—Jamie Fiore Higgins, author of *Bully Market: My Story of Money and Misogyny at Goldman Sachs*

"*Tread Loudly* is an empowering book that every young woman attorney (or aspiring attorney) needs on her shelf. Bursting with practical, actionable strategies and invaluable insights infused with real-life experience and humor, this must-read will empower you to tackle the unique challenges faced by women in the legal profession with confidence."

—Katie Day Winchenbach, Program Director, Ms. JD

Tread
LOUDLY

Tread
LOUDLY

Call Out the Bullsh*t and Fight
for Equality in the Workplace

Kristine Cherek

BrainTrust
INK

BrainTrust Ink
Nashville, Tennessee
www.braintrustink.com

Distributed by Greenleaf Book Group

For ordering information or special discounts for bulk purchases, please contact Greenleaf Book Group at PO Box 91869, Austin, TX 78709, 512.891.6100.

Design and composition by Greenleaf Book Group and Sheila Parr
Cover design by Greenleaf Book Group and Sheila Parr
Cover image used under license from ©TheNounProject/Hayley Parke

Publisher's Cataloging-in-Publication data is available.

Print ISBN: 978-1-956072-17-4

eBook ISBN: 978-1-956072-18-1

To offset the number of trees consumed in the printing of our books, Greenleaf donates a portion of the proceeds from each printing to the Arbor Day Foundation. Greenleaf Book Group has replaced over 50,000 trees since 2007.

Printed in the United States of America on acid-free paper

23 24 25 26 27 28   10 9 8 7 6 5 4 3 2 1

First Edition

For the young women of the next generation, especially

Amanda Rose, Amanda Linn, Emma Mae, Elizabeth, Casey,
Sarah, Sophia, Baby Mae, Morgan, Kenzie, and Lindsey.

You are my inspiration. You are my reason. I want the world
to be a better, easier, and more equitable place for you and for
all the young women and girls who will come after you.

Love, Aunt Kristine

Contents

Preface xiii

Introduction 1

Chapter 1: Putting in the Work 7

Chapter 2: Figuring Out Your Why 21

Chapter 3: If You Could Do Anything, What Would It Be? 35

Chapter 4: There Is No Such Thing as "Having It All" 45

Chapter 5: Representation Matters 69

Chapter 6: Don't Let Their Judgments Define You 83

Chapter 7: Confronting Locker Room Talk 93

Chapter 8: Speak Your Truth 101

Chapter 9: It Takes More Than Grit 117

Chapter 10: Quitting Is Not Failure 137

Chapter 11: Where Do We Go from Here? 149

Acknowledgments 159

Notes 165

About the Author 171

Preface

I am used to being the only woman in the room. Over the years, I got used to people assuming I was someone's assistant, secretary (as the older men called me), or paralegal. I've been called "sweetheart," "young lady," "girl," "honey," and similar names more times than I can count. I'm used to people underestimating my intellect and ability. I'm used to people treating me differently simply because I'm a woman.

I spent the last two decades building my career in male-dominated workplaces and male-dominated industries. Young attorney, corporate vice president, law firm partner, professor—I've been each of these things in my career (so far). Along the way, I've been through more than my share of struggles and, for the most part, came out on the other side. And I want to share what I've learned with you.

Throughout my career, I often wished I had a mentor, a guide, someone who would let me peek behind the curtain to see what her life was *really* like. To share what she struggled with and how she dealt with it. To validate that what I was feeling was normal and justified. To be a friend, a sister-in-arms, someone to commiserate with, someone to laugh with, and a real-life example of a professional woman who struggled like hell and succeeded despite those struggles—perhaps even because of those struggles. To be real. And brutally honest.

If you, too, wish you had that person, or if you might be that person for someone else, this book may be for you.

Despite having had many of the experiences, run-ins, thoughts, ideas, and soapbox arguments that I talk about in this book throughout my career, there is no way I could have written it before now. Until now, I lacked the clarity and confidence to speak up. Until now, I did not have the time or mental bandwidth to reflect on any of this, let alone do something about it. Now I do.

Over the years I had several almost-constant thoughts:

1. Am I the only one who feels disillusioned and lost in the corporate world? Is anyone else dismayed by what they're experiencing?

2. This (the white male-centric culture) does not seem right. Does anyone else agree?

3. Balancing my career with my family, friends, personal life, and self is *hard*. Really hard. Maybe impossible. Everyone else seems to have it under control. Am I the only one struggling?

4. It is not okay that my coworkers (whether they outrank me or not) treat me differently because of my gender. It is not okay that any of my coworkers are treated differently because of their race, ethnicity, national origin, gender identity, gender expression, sexual orientation, religion, disability, or age. Any "ism," no matter how minor or veiled, is not okay.

5. I should be able to succeed in the corporate world without having to disguise, hide, or abandon who I am. The same is true for *all* my coworkers.

6. The world needs to know what is happening in the workplace and in our society in general. Someone needs to tell these stories. Someone needs to shine a light on all of this.

To be successful, I had to quietly endure at least some amount of gender bias. Over the years I struggled, sometimes a lot, to balance my career with my family, friends, personal life, and self. I had to assimilate with the corporate culture as much as possible. I had to abandon at least some of myself to become what the world already expected me to be. I had to dim my light in order to fit into a predetermined role in society. I had to find a way to exist within the power structure in order to keep playing the game.

I was (wrongly) taught there was one set path to success, and that path necessitated disguising what made me different or unique. I was (wrongly) told I needed to make people forget my gender, my differences, and most of all the fact that I had a life outside of work. I (wrongly) believed the fight for gender equality in the corporate world had largely been won by the generations of women who came before me.

I now know all of that is bullshit.

The truth is, I had to keep quiet in order to climb the career ladder. The corporate world was not yet ready or able to listen to loud voices demanding equal treatment. We, the Gen-X women who built our careers in the dawn of the new millennium, became the bridge between the Baby Boomer days of male-dominated, *Mad Men*–like workplaces and today's fight for true equality. We needed to take baby steps and tiptoe around. We needed to change corporate cultures bit by bit, so those in power would not even realize it was happening. Quiet, slow progress was the only way. We needed to tread lightly, quietly, and within the constraints imposed upon us by the power structures. But that was then, and this is now.

I want the women of the next generation to do the exact opposite. And I want to help you get there. I wrote this book because I feel
compelled to bring these issues to light. I want the people in my
life—and in the world in general—to know what my friends and I
endured and what too many women continue to endure even today.

I want women, and especially the Millennial and Gen-Z generations of women and girls, to know you are not alone. I don't want you
to feel the way I felt or experience what I have gone through. I want
you to be empowered to stand up and speak out against the biases and
the wrongs that occur, whether gigantic or seemingly tiny. I want you
to know you are equally important irrespective of your gender, marital
status, or whether you have children. And while my experiences are
based on my identity and role in the world as a cisgender female (and
I can only speak from that knowledge point), I am acutely aware that
the struggles do not end with the categorizations of male or female,
married or not, parent or not. While it may be beyond my experience and what I can advocate for in the limited number of pages in
one book, let me be clear: I want the corporate world to value you
and treat you as equally important irrespective of your race, ethnicity,
national origin, gender identity, gender expression, sexual orientation, religion, disability, and age. You matter equally. You should not
have to encounter bias, inequity, or any amount of harassment or
discrimination in the workplace (or in the world in general, but that's
a broader topic for another day).

I want you to know it will sometimes be a struggle. But you'll be
okay. You'll be better than okay. Life is messy for all of us, even those
who are really good at hiding it. Together we can make this crazy,
stressful, unfair, messy thing called life better for all of us. And it starts
with each of us telling our truths.

I hope this book will serve as a resource and a refuge for you.
I want you to know you are not alone. I want you to know your

struggles are common. I want you to know you do not have to endure the type of gender bias that women who are now in their forties and fifties endured when they first started out. While I can only speak to my experiences of facing gender bias, the principles apply equally to other biases. I want you to know you have the power and the right to speak up for who you are and what is important to you. You have not only the power to change your own life, but you also have the power to change the workplace culture for those who will come after you.

I hope you'll find some humor in the daily struggles of me and my friends. I hope you will find some collegiality in knowing what others have gone through (and in many respects, continue to go through). I hope you will find some inspiration. I hope you'll feel at least a little bit of disbelief when reading some of the true tales of things that happened "back then." I hope you'll even feel a little bit of outrage surrounding the state of the world for working women today. Lastly, I hope you will feel compelled to call out the bullshit and fight for real change. For yourself. For others to come. For all of us.

Introduction

Don't try to squeeze into a glass slipper.
Instead, shatter the glass ceiling.

—PRIYANKA CHOPRA JONAS

As a little girl, I didn't dress up in princess costumes. I could not envision my future wedding. I wasn't interested in Barbies or baby dolls, and I didn't dream of the day my prince would come. Instead, I dreamed of courtrooms, boardrooms, and corner offices. There would be no glass slippers in my future. Unless, of course, the glass slippers were designed by Christian Louboutin, and I bought them for myself.

I was raised by a Gloria Steinem–loving, unapologetic feminist mom. Hers was not an enviable position. She was a divorced mom with three young girls in the 1970s and 1980s—an era in which *no one* in our community was divorced. She made it her life's mission to raise her daughters to be educated, strong, and independent. There were no Disney princess movies, no pink bedrooms, and no lace dresses in our house. We read *Little Women* and watched movies about the civil rights movement. I got home from school most afternoons to find math worksheets waiting for me on the kitchen table. These were not homework, per se. These were store-bought workbooks, completely unrelated to my actual schoolwork, that my mother convinced me were more fun than playing with toys. From my early childhood memories, I can still hear her saying, "You should be a lawyer when you grow up." While she indulged my love of Cabbage Patch Kids (I was a child of the 1980s, after all), she made sure to balance out the baby dolls with books, basketballs, and big dreams.

When I wanted to take ballet classes as a little girl, my mother signed me up for softball instead. I hated softball. She made me play anyway, at least until I was old enough to defy her and outright refuse. We finally compromised and settled on gymnastics: still powerful and strong (for her), but graceful and sparkly (for me).

Striving for perfection

I started tumbling class before I started kindergarten. By the time I was eight, I was spending five days a week at the gym. I didn't have friends at school or in my neighborhood. The gym was my home. My teammates were my only friends. It was the place where I felt comfortable. It was the place where I belonged. It was the place where things made sense. You work hard, you do what you are told, you follow the rules, you make progress, and eventually you achieve what you are working toward. Through the influence of my mom and my very intense gymnastics coaches, I was raised to be tough, aggressive, and confident. I was raised not to cry when I fell off the balance beam. I was trained to push through frustration and challenges. I was conditioned like a little robot to get up off the ground and try again. I pushed through tears and through injuries, always keeping my eye on the bigger goal. One season when I had a cast on my hand to protect broken bones, I still went to the gym every day. There was always something that could be learned, muscles that could be trained, and skills that could be perfected, even as a gymnast with only one available hand.

I was raised to think perfection is possible if you work hard enough. I was trained to understand, even at a very young age, that success is the reward for painfully hard work. I was raised to believe that people—and even little girls—are powerful, fierce, and can achieve anything they dream of if they put in the hard work.

It is probably no surprise that my life didn't follow the traditional route for a baby girl born in the 1970s. Attorney, corporate vice president, professor. In the two-plus decades of my professional life, I have been each of these things. I've learned a lot along the way. Most importantly, I've been lucky enough to find and surround myself with some pretty amazing people.

I began my career as a young corporate attorney at one of the top one hundred largest law firms in the United States. In the legal world, these firms are called the "Am Law 100" because of the rankings published by a legal news site called the *American Lawyer*. Statistically, the halls of the Am Law 100 are filled predominantly with people who are white, affluent, who identify as male, and who are heterosexual.[1] I had to learn pretty quickly how to acclimate to an environment that was very different from the one in which I was raised. Over time, I found my people (sometimes through trial and error) and began to build my career. I later joined a real estate development company, then took a trip back to a big firm, and eventually landed at a university. In each phase of my career, I met some incredible people who became not only my colleagues but also my confidants, mentors, teachers, sources of support, and true friends.

My (very accomplished) girlfriends

I count among my close friends some very accomplished women: the chief operating officer of a Major League Baseball team, the hiring partner of an international law firm, two college professors, two Fortune 500 company executives, and a creative whose designs include iconic sports arenas and music venues across the Midwest.

By all measures, these women seem to have found a way to have it all (if you believe in the fallacy that "having it all" is even possible). They have accomplished careers, happy families, strong relationships, fulfilling friendships, and even social lives. Their designer clothes are neatly pressed. Their houses are clean. Their children (for those who have children) are clean and *polite*. They serve on nonprofit boards and host fundraising galas. The walls of their offices are lined with awards that mark their professional accomplishments. And, from an outsider's view, they make it all look *so easy*.

How is this possible? Do these people have more hours in a day than the rest of us? Have they figured out how to pause time? Do they have an invisible army helping them? Did they clone themselves? Did they make a deal with the devil in exchange for their seemingly perfect lives?

I think my girlfriends would be okay with me letting you in on a little secret. They are not perfect. In fact, they are far from perfect. They are not superheroes, at least not in the traditional sense. They have not discovered some miracle solution to being an overstressed, overworked, overcommitted, and overtired adult. They have not escaped inequality, inequity, sexism, or bias in their professional lives. Rather, they are regular humans who are doing their best on a daily basis to juggle their careers, families, friends, and selves. They strive to do it with integrity and, hopefully, in a way that makes the path easier for the next generation. Their lives are a delicate construct of looming client deadlines, carpool schedules, demanding bosses, indispensable assistants, color-coded calendars, supportive partners, helpful parents, friends who save the day, takeout dinners, and Amazon Prime deliveries. Lots of Amazon Prime deliveries.

Through trial and error, with perseverance, and in most instances without someone to guide us, my girlfriends and I figured out how to survive—and even succeed—in the corporate world. I want to share some of the lessons we learned, with the hope that it helps you avoid some of the mistakes we committed and inspires you to build on the progress we've made so far in the fight for equality.

What to expect in the pages that follow

Some of what follows are the experiences, advice, commentaries, and true stories of the women of my (forty- and fiftysomething) generation. These are not tales of historic accomplishment. Rather, these are true accounts of things that actually happened in the lives of my friends and me. A few are memoirs written at pivotal points in time. Others are recitations of the mundane struggle to keep our shit together on a daily basis. They are the lessons we learned, the advice we wish someone had shared with us decades ago, the knowledge we gained, and the puzzles we figured out along the way. They are the true tales of the inequities and inequalities we still navigate. They are commentaries on the issues that demand our collective attention, and hopefully they are the push we need to make our voices heard. Loudly.

I promised anonymity in exchange for the right to tell some of these stories. To that end, most of the names (other than my husband's and mine) and some identifying facts have been changed. But the underlying stories are very real. So read on, learn from us, laugh with us, laugh at us, have a drink with us, feel a little outrage alongside us, and realize that even those who appear to have it all figured out are, in reality, struggling to keep it together. Every. Single. Day.

The bottom line

There are no magic answers. There are no shortcuts. There is no bulletproof advice I can give you that will fix your life. We haven't solved all of this country's gender equality problems. I am sorry to report that unicorns don't exist. But there *are* lessons that can be learned from our struggles. There are mistakes that can be avoided. There are truths we can share. There are issues and inequities that demand our attention. And there is comfort in knowing you are not alone in the struggle to manage this precious, complicated thing called life. There are lessons we all have to learn the hard way. But maybe, just maybe, you will find some insight, wisdom, comfort, outrage, and inspiration in what follows. The truth is pretty simple: we are all just trying, learning, evolving, and figuring life out, one day at a time.

1

Putting in the Work

I strongly believe if you work hard, whatever you want,
it will come to you. I know that's easier
said than done, but keep trying.

—BEYONCÉ

Imagine yourself reduced to the size of a single Cheerio. You are a beautiful Cheerio, unique in your shape, size, and texture. There is nothing in the world exactly like you. You've worked your entire life to stand out from the crowd. Your parents and teachers always told you that you are special, you are smart, and you will achieve great things. You are filled with ambition and ready to take on the world.

Now imagine being poured into a giant bowl along with hundreds of other Cheerios. As you look around, you quickly realize you aren't so special after all. The others are accomplished. They have unique talents. They are intelligent. Some are utterly brilliant. You find it harder and harder to stand out from the crowd. Suddenly you find yourself drowning in a bowl of other Cheerios, every one of which is just as unique and special as you are.

Welcome to your adult life.

You're an adult . . . now what?

The working world is an intimidating place. You are bound to be a little (or a lot) unnerved, especially in the early years of your career. That's okay. That's normal. Everyone else is intimidated, too. They are just better at hiding it. You are going to have doubts. You are going to think everyone is smarter than you are. Some days you will wonder whether you can even survive this place. Everything will be okay in the end. You will make it through this. I promise. There are a few things I would like to tell you—things I wish I had known back in the early years of my career.

For me, the harsh reality of adulthood hit during my first semester of law school. I realize law school is not exactly the "real" world, but it felt pretty real to me. The weight of responsibility, uncertainty, and the Imposter Syndrome I felt as a new law student was very much the same as what my friends outside of law school were going through. While my experience is graduate school–centric, the lessons I learned apply regardless of whether you are a software developer, doctor, investment banker, or salesperson. Adulthood strikes no matter who you are, where you come from, or how hard you try to postpone or avoid it. Trust me, I've tried.

My humble start

When I arrived at the University of Wisconsin Law School, I came armed with a lifetime of good grades, a long resume of extracurricular activities, and the naïve ambition of a toddler. I was a bright, talented, special Cheerio who would certainly rise to the top. Or would I? Seen differently, I was a twenty-two-year-old former college cheerleader from a good-but-not-Ivy-League university. I had zero professional work experience. My Midwestern, blue-collar accent gave away my somewhat humble upbringing.

I was raised in a working-class neighborhood by a working-class family. My parents got divorced before I started kindergarten. From my earliest memories into high school, I was the *only kid* with divorced parents. I was the only kid with divorced parents in my neighborhood, my schools, my church, my ballet classes, and my gymnastics team. The "divorced parents" label made me especially unique (not in a good way) at the all-girls Catholic high school I attended. Maybe I got comfortable being the only woman in so many conference rooms and boardrooms full of men because I was used to the feeling of being different. People could try to pretend it didn't matter. But in many of their eyes, my otherness was obvious.

Back in the 1970s and 1980s, there was no such thing as shared custody. Kids of divorced parents lived with their mother, while the divorced dad worked to pay the bills for two households and occasionally attended school concerts and birthday parties. And so that's how life went for me from kindergarten through high school. Where I grew up, children were raised with the help of extended family, regardless of whether one or both parents were around. In that sense, my family wasn't so different from any other. Families were close, and I don't just mean that in an emotional sense.

Three of my mother's siblings lived within six blocks of us. All had lived in that same zip code since birth. Ditto for my father's brother. My paternal grandparents lived eight blocks away in the same house where they raised my father a generation before. My mom's mom lived a whopping 1.8 miles away. Geographically, our world was small, and we rarely ventured outside of its boundaries. We were a people who were born, raised, and lived in the same neighborhood with the same neighbors for our entire lives. Ours was the kind of town where you would walk into the local pizzeria to find the founder's grandkids running the joint and my best friend's dad behind the bar serving drinks. It was the kind of town where everyone knows you—and three generations of your family. I met someone recently who said, "You're Dewey's daughter, right?" To be clear, I am a grown adult and my dad passed away over a decade ago. But in my old neighborhood, I will always be Dewey's daughter. Proudly.

There was a pattern to our lives: Attend the same elementary school and high school that our parents and grandparents attended, graduate (or not), secure a decent job that pays a decent wage, and make a life in the same neighborhood in which we were born and raised. Simply put, we worked hard, took pride in our jobs, loved our families, followed the rules, and lived a nice life. We never desired too much or stretched too far beyond our boundaries.

Growing up, though, I could not wait to get the hell out of there. This place is too small, I thought. Too gritty. Too close-knit. Too *everything*. I was determined to make my life different. My older sister was the first person on either side of my extended family to attend college. Eight years later, I was the second. We were the outliers, the different ones, the ones who didn't fit in. We had big dreams. And those dreams led my sister all the way to a PhD, and me to law school.

Reality—and feelings of inferiority—set in

While I had the academic credentials needed for admission, to say I was comfortable in my new role as a law student would be a massive misstatement. My sister was not only the first person in my extended family to attend college; she was also the only person I'd ever known who had done so. I was like a mermaid out of water.

I might have looked like everyone else but I felt like I was walking on land for the first time. My work experience as a part-time receptionist at my father's small business was not going to impress my professors. Or anyone else. I was going to have to find my way in this scary new world filled with so many intelligent, motivated, and accomplished people.

As I met my new colleagues, I quickly realized that most were older than me. Many were married and seemed like real, actual, grown-up people. They owned houses. Some even had children. I didn't even have a boyfriend. Most had been in the professional world for at least a few years, many working as accountants, bankers, and paralegals. A few had even worked on Capitol Hill. The totality of my work experience included answering phones, typing and filing, and coaching cheerleading. Some of my classmates were descended from multiple generations of attorneys. Neither of my parents had the opportunity to even dream of a college education.

My confidence as a special Cheerio quickly evaporated. I immediately doubted everything I had believed to be true (i.e., that I was intelligent, worthy, and destined for big things). After finishing the first week of classes, I was convinced I was the *only one* who had no idea what was going on. I was *absolutely sure* every single person was smarter than me. I was *positive* I would fail. I did my best to hide in class and avoid being called on. I knew it was only a matter of time before my ineptness would be revealed to all.

Putting in the work

A funny thing happened on my way to failure: I didn't fail at all. I succeeded. Not because I was destined to, or because I was particularly brilliant. I succeeded because I put in the hard work. Terrified during those first few weeks, I pledged to entirely commit myself to school for one year. I would do almost nothing but eat, breathe, sleep, and study. I would give my classes everything I had. If my everything was not good enough, then so be it. I could go back to my old neighborhood and the life I knew knowing that I'd given it my best shot.

I did not make any friends in those years except for one similarly young and intimidated girl who became my study partner, my roommate, my coworker, and eventually the maid of honor at my wedding. I did not join a single student organization. I did not attend a single happy hour, social event, or anything else that was not directly tied to a graded component of one of my courses. I ruthlessly guarded my time. I studied. And studied. Then studied more. Obviously not everyone has the luxury to be so self-absorbed. I cannot say I recommend this level of isolationism to anyone. But it worked for me.

You're not the only one

Nearly two decades later, as a professor, I welcomed my students as they entered their first class of their first semester. Later, I coached them as they interviewed for their first professional jobs, and I proudly watched as they began their careers. I saw in my students' faces the same looks of confusion that I know filled my face years prior. I saw the confident ones. I saw the terrified ones. I saw the ones who didn't believe in themselves even though I believed in them. Whereas twenty years ago I thought I was the *only one* who did not understand what was going on, decades later I saw that the vast majority of my students felt the *exact same way*. If any young professional believes she has a good grasp of her chosen field or thinks she is very good at her job, then she is either exceptional or sadly mistaken. As for the rest of us newbies, fear not; it will all begin to make sense in due time.

Students often asked me, "How did you get to where you are?" It felt like they were looking for a magical answer, some map to point them to the promised land, or the secret to success. There is no magic bullet other than this: you need to put in the hard work to get the results.

One of my good friends during my undergrad years mastered the art of maximal performance on minimal effort. That is a nice way of saying she didn't pay much attention to the "student" part of being a college student. She rarely studied. She refused to register for classes that began before 11:00 a.m. Even then, she sometimes slept through her classes. She spent more time watching movies with her boyfriend than she did in class and studying combined. She only bought the textbooks for some of her courses. Other times she "purchased" the text the day before the final exam, studied for one night, then returned the text in time to meet the bookstore's twenty-four-hour return policy. She reasoned that, if she could get B or C grades by putting in minimal effort, it was not worth the time or work to go for the A. She subscribed to the saying that "Cs equal degrees." For naturally intelligent students like my friend, this approach may have worked through college. But let me be clear: minimal effort is simply not going to cut it in the real world.

Toto, we aren't in college anymore.

Settling into work life

Life in the working world is tiring, especially during the early years. Sometimes it is exhausting. And honestly, it can get mundane. Gone are the days of having a fresh start to each semester. Gone are the midterm breaks, spring breaks and, of course, summer breaks. There is no clean slate, no fresh start, no chance to reinvent yourself every few months. The corporate world can make you feel like a hamster running on a wheel: you keep running and running, and the wheel keeps spinning and spinning, but you never actually go anywhere. No matter what stage of your career you are in, please know you are getting somewhere. Even when it feels like you're running on a treadmill, you are getting somewhere. All of the hard work will pay off in the end. Have faith.

In the early years of your career, most of your coworkers will be older than you. That can be intimidating as hell. Please do not view youth or inexperience as a negative. You may not have the years of experience that some of your coworkers do, but your ideas, your creativity, your energy, and your approach to life are positive attributes that some of your older coworkers will probably lack. And you are every bit as intelligent as they are. Do not be intimidated by others' past accomplishments. None of that matters now. The only things that matter are how you perform today and what you accomplish next. So put your head down and work hard. Do not even think about what others are doing or how you stack up against them. Worry only about yourself. After all, that is all you can really control.

There is no way to sugarcoat this: The workload in the corporate world is heavy at times. And if I'm being honest, sometimes the work can be pretty boring. Your manager (or boss, team leader, or whatever term your company uses) will be tough on you. Some will have Draconian policies that lack practical sense. Some will be theoretical, if not actual, ogres. At times it will seem like they thrive on being unfairly harsh to you. Try not to take it personally. Try to use it as fuel for your internal fire.

Don't let anyone tell you that you can't do it

In my first semester of law school, I was told by an elderly professor that I was "too young and naïve" to be in his class; that perhaps the admissions committee made a mistake in admitting "someone as idealistic" as me. He said I better realize life is not fair or I'd have little chance of survival in the real world. He said this in response to some impromptu, off-the-cuff answer I gave when he called on me in class one day. I don't remember his question, my answer, or even the topic we were discussing. But I remember his opinion of me. Vividly.

When he said these words to me, out loud, in a lecture hall filled with my new classmates, I could feel my face burning, the tears welling up in my eyes, and the rage inside of me rising. I wanted to disappear into the wood of the uncomfortable seat upon which I sat. Somehow, I fought back the tears and held it together in that moment. Maybe it was all those years of gymnastics training. Do not cry, I would tell myself each time my gymnastics coach would tell me to do it *again*, and do it *right* this time. Maybe all that training was coming back to me, or maybe I was just too stunned to do anything but sit in a speechless stupor.

After my immediate desire to quit law school subsided, I came up with a different plan. I vowed to prove him wrong. I made it my goal to graduate (with honors) so I could tell him just how wrong he had been about me.

I realized later his words were not an indictment. They were only one person's misinformed opinion of me based on very little information. What did he really know about me beyond my name and the one answer I'd given that he decided to judge me on? He didn't know my background, my life experiences, my determination, or how smart (or not) I was. He had no idea who I really was, what drove me, or what my future potential might be. So how could he judge me? More importantly, how could I let that judgment invade my confidence and raise my self-doubt? The more I thought about it, the more it didn't make sense.

I realized people will judge us, sometimes harshly, based on very little information. It is our choice what to do with that judgment. We can let it seep into our brains and tarnish our self-confidence. Or we can ignore it altogether. Or, as I did, we can use it to motivate ourselves.

Every time I wanted to give up, quit, or say I've had enough, I thought about the satisfaction I would get from walking across the stage on graduation day, with a smile on my face and my diploma in hand. I thought about how good it would feel to prove this old, grumpy, jaded person wrong.

In some small way, I now understand what my professor was trying to accomplish. Yes, his tactics were overly harsh and probably subconsciously sexist. (Would he have told a similarly aged male student he was too young and naïve? I seriously doubt it.) But his intent may have been in the right place. Professors, at least the ones I know now, do not like to embarrass students for the sake of embarrassment alone. Their burden is heavy. It is their task, of course, to teach. But it is also their duty to prepare their students for the realities of the working world. It was that professor's job to transform me, a twenty-two-year-old girl with zero professional work experience, into a future graduate worthy of her well-paid and important-sounding position at a major company. Bosses and professors take their jobs very seriously. Hate them now. But thank them later.

I still believe my professor's tactics were wrong. But he probably sensed I would need to toughen up if I was going to succeed in the corporate world. Hopefully you will never encounter a boss, manager, team leader, or CEO who treats you with such disdain. But if you do, I hope you will remember my story and use the experience as fuel for your future success.

Find your people

Surviving life in any workplace can be a challenge. In the first few years you will meet a lot of people. Look for one named Marti. Like you, Marti is young, ambitious, and a little nervous. While there is no way you could know this when you meet her, Marti will become your coworker, friend, confidant, and constant companion. She will be your voice of reason, sounding board, and shoulder to cry on when you need it. Trust me, you will need it if you are going to make it through the tough years of your career with your sanity in check.

I met my Marti on the first day of law school orientation. I was immediately drawn to her because, like me, she stood out from the mostly older, mostly professional-looking crowd. We both looked like we had stepped off the set of *Friends*, with our miniskirts and matching tights, cropped sweaters, and Mary Jane chunky-heeled shoes. While my mom taught me to never judge someone by her outward appearance, I knew Marti and I were destined to become best friends the minute I saw her. It wasn't just the way we were dressed. She looked serious. And determined. And to be honest, a little scared. I felt *all of that*. We were intimidated, ambitious young women faking our way in a scary new phase of life.

We bonded over contract law and acrylic nails in the weeks and months that followed. The more I got to know her, the more I realized she was exactly what I needed: Someone who was going through the same scary thing as me, someone I could confide in, someone I could be honest with in sharing how underqualified I felt, and someone who was as serious about her future goals as I was. For the next few years, we took the same classes, studied together, and lived together. We blocked out the distractions, kept to ourselves, avoided the social scene, and studied. Then we studied some more. Our refuge from the books came on Monday nights when we watched *Melrose Place* and devoured a family size pizza. This became such a ritual that the delivery guy knew our names and our exact order. I wish I was kidding about that part.

Marti and I landed summer internships, and eventually coveted permanent job offers, from the same firm (albeit three floors apart, with her joining the litigation team and me joining the corporate law team). We were classmates, friends, roommates, and coworkers. In the early days of our careers, we relied on each other, leaned on one another, supported each other in the difficult times, and celebrated each other on the good days. We still do. It isn't an overstatement to say I don't know how I would've made it through my twenties and thirties without her. While our careers and lives took us in different directions (literally and figuratively), and while we don't get to see each other very often now that we live on opposite sides of the country, Marti and I will always be each other's people.

Not everyone is lucky enough to find their Marti. But everyone should try.

Look for someone like you. Someone who is going through the same thing you are. Someone who has similar dreams and career goals as you. One who shares your determination and your work ethic. Someone who has the same level of commitment to her career as you. Find that person (or if you are really lucky, those people) and hang on tightly. Those people are rare and precious.

Make friends in your professional life, but not too many. Go for quality, not quantity. Those early years of your work life can be rough. You are going to need a friend—a real friend—to help you through the stress that is inherently there. Try to find your Marti because you are going to need her. And she is going to need you.

Adulting is hard—but you'll be okay

The professional world is challenging, inspiring, stressful, tiring, exciting, energizing, monotonous, and boring all at once. Please know it is okay if you feel intimidated, apprehensive, underqualified, in over your head, or unsure of yourself. It is okay even if you feel ALL of these things. While everyone feels this way at times, almost no one admits it. That, my friends, is the big secret of young adulthood. So many people are "faking it until they make it" that we all believe we are the only ones who don't have it all figured out. We all feel the Imposter Syndrome creep in, even those of us who have been at this game for decades.

When you doubt yourself (and it's going to happen), think back to my stories. Think back to how I felt during my college and post-college years. No one (outside of my parents and Marti) had any idea how out of place I felt. No one knew I was sure I was doomed to fail. No one would've believed how clueless I really was. My face didn't reveal it. My actions didn't show it. I was playing the game just like everyone else. Only I didn't know everyone else was playing too. To the outside world, it looked like I had everything under control. But inside, I was always just one step away from thinking the house of cards was about to collapse, leaving everyone to know what an imposter I was. But that never happened. I kept pretending (to my classmates and later my coworkers) that everything was fine until, eventually, everything actually *was* fine.

The wrap up

The key to success early in your career is, in my opinion, pretty simple. Always keep your eye on the ball. Work hard. Pay close attention to what the successful people around you are doing and emulate that. Seek out mentors, whether within your company or industry or outside of it. Find what works for you and stick to it. Ignore the noise that permeates the hallways, the water coolers, and social media. Do not fall victim to the distractions of the social scene. Guard your time. Help your colleagues, but not at the expense of your own success. Work hard. Then work harder. Have confidence to know you can—and you will—be successful.

Learn from those who have gone before you. Keep reading because you just might learn some things that will help you along the way. Take these lessons to heart. My friends and I spent the past two-plus decades struggling through our professional lives. We figured some things out and we want to share those truths with you. No one is perfect. No one is infallible. Everyone has a competitive edge. Your task is to find yours, then use it to your advantage. You have a very limited amount of time in which to make your mark and build your career. Approach every day as if the rest of your career depends on it. Because it does.

KEY TAKEAWAYS

- There are no shortcuts to success. Trust that your hard work will pay off over time, even if it might not feel like it in the moment. Stay focused and vigilant about your goals.

- Do not let others' opinions of you diminish your belief in yourself. What someone else thinks about you is not your concern.

- Don't listen to anyone who tells you that you can't do it (whatever it is). Use their doubt to fuel your motivation.

- We all feel intimidated, underqualified, or like we have no idea what we are doing at times. You are not the only one who sometimes feels like an imposter.

2

Figuring Out Your Why

Picture the job you dreamed you'd have. Are you living the life you envisioned for yourself? Are you who you wanted to be when you grew up? Or are you still dreaming of something even bigger?

—MEREDITH GREY, *GREY'S ANATOMY*

"It is like a cake eating contest where the prize is more cake." That was my mentor's very accurate description of what life is like after you get the big promotion . . . when you finally land the job you have been dreaming of.

It was the mid-2000s and I was a young(ish) person in career distress. Mathematically, I was probably past the quarter-life point in my existence on this planet, absent some pretty major advances in science. But what I was going through felt like a full-on, raging, undeniable, quarter-life crisis.

From an outsider's perspective, it probably looked like I had everything under control. I had worked my ass off for the prior seven years, moving up the ranks with one promotion, then another. I was running the company's summer internship program on top of my regular workload. I was logging more hours than most of my peers (which, according to that company's culture, meant that I was "winning"). I was staffed on projects for some of the company's biggest clients, the kinds of things you'd read about in the news. All indications were that I was on track for the big promotion, the one I had been working toward since the day I first stepped into the place. All I had to do was keep doing what I was doing, keep working my butt off, put in another few "short" years, and then it would all pay off. Everything was going exactly according to plan. At least that's what it looked like from the outside.

My existential career crisis

Silently, though, I was having a career crisis of the existential kind.

Did I really want the big promotion? Or was I pursuing it out of some competitive need to capture the prize? Did I want to keep working a crazy number of hours, every week, for years to come? For forever? Or would I be happier in a career with a better work/life balance? Would I rather have the kind of job that left me time to do my laundry and iron my own clothes? Would I even want to go to my nieces' dance recitals if I weren't working every Saturday? And what did it even look like to eat dinner together as a family on a regular basis? That world was entirely foreign to me.

For the prior seven-plus years, my only focus had been on my career. Luckily for me, my husband, Kirk, felt the exact same way about his work. We were a match made in productivity culture heaven.

Then, little by little, the questions started to creep into my mind. Did I thrive on the thrill of the work? Or was I just doing all of this for the prestige? Did I really want the big promotion? Or did I just think I wanted it because everyone else did? Most importantly, would my life suddenly change for the better once I landed the big promotion?

I'm lucky that I had a great mentor who was always willing to work through my latest crisis with me. He listened, patiently, while I ran through every iteration that had been brewing in my mind. He allowed me to vent, hypothesize, guess, get mad, and generally freak out from time to time. He knew how to calm me down. He wouldn't just tell me what I wanted to hear; he would tell me what I *needed* to hear, no matter how hard that sometimes was to digest on the receiving end. He had been through the process and now occupied a seat at the table I was striving to sit at. And he was brutally honest about what life was really like for him and his peers.

I realize that not everyone has a senior mentor they can turn to for advice. The real, honest, unfiltered kind. I was lucky enough to come across one person in my work life who was that to me. Only one person. Ever. In over twenty years. So, if you have not found that person yet, allow me to do the honors. While my experience is in the legal and corporate worlds, the lessons learned apply equally to any profession. Please read on, laugh at my ignorance, marvel at my naïvete, and take comfort in knowing no one could possibly be as clueless as I once was. (And I still turned out okay. At least I think I did.)

Being the boss is . . . just okay

I had this naïve conception early in my career that life must be *so much better* once one gets the big promotion. Life must be *so much easier* for the boss (or manager, team leader, supervisor, director, or whatever title your company uses). For me, the boss was called a partner. And partners, I figured, had it all. I wanted that for myself. I wanted it so badly. Or at least I thought I did. But did I really want it at all?

In my state of ignorance, I figured that partners are the experts; therefore, they must know everything, or at least everything they need to know to do their jobs really well. They must not get intimidated or stumped by any problem thrown their way. They must feel as confident as they appear. They must have everything under control. They must have a handle on their work schedules and therefore their lives. The pressure must not get to them after all those years.

Turns out, none of that is true. It takes years—sometimes even decades—to master any set of skills. Even Simone Biles, generally thought to be the greatest gymnast of all time, still had a lot to learn after winning four consecutive national championship titles. She still had more to accomplish, more national, world, and Olympic titles to win, and more skills to perfect. And, as we all witnessed at the 2020 Olympics, even Simone Biles loses confidence in herself at times. Being the best doesn't make one infallible or all-knowing, and it doesn't give one unwavering confidence.

The same is true in every other sport, every industry, and every profession. Even the pros, the ones who make it all look so easy, are learning new skills, trying new approaches, and overcoming moments in which they lack confidence. What makes us think that we—the regular, non-world-class-level people—would be any different?

I wish I could say that landing the big promotion you've been dreaming of makes everything right with the world. I wish I could tell you the clouds will clear, the angels will sing, and a bright light will shine down on you. I wish I could say that the people in charge have really manageable schedules. I wish I could tell you they do not work weekends, their dinners don't get interrupted with phone calls, and they never have to postpone a vacation. I wish I could say their clients are all really nice people who never demand completely unreasonable things. But those would be lies.

It is important to acknowledge that getting the big promotion is not everyone's dream. We don't all set our sights on becoming the boss. But it is the right thing for some people. Some of us inherently know this is our chosen path; others of us inherently know it is not. Having a clear vision of what you do or do not want is, I think, the most enviable state of being. If you are happy with where you are and don't desire to move upward in your career, I genuinely mean it when I say good for you. You know yourself well enough to make that determination. You get to avoid the existential career crisis that burdened me. If you are certain you want to keep climbing the career ladder, I genuinely say good for you as well. Keep pursuing your goals while keeping your eyes wide open about what being at the top of the career pyramid truly entails.

If you are somewhere in the messy middle (as I was), please know you are not alone. I've been there. In many ways, I am still there and always will be. For many of us, figuring out what we truly want is the most difficult quest of all. It is a lifelong, constantly evolving reexamination of self and our goals, wants, and priorities. And that's okay. That's more than okay; that's being human. Maybe, just maybe, my story and my insights will help bring into focus for others what it is they truly want. Maybe it will help you figure out your why.

Not all paths run straight

You may have gleaned from the parts of my story you've read so far that my path to landing the big title wasn't linear. I did not join one company upon graduation, work my way up the ranks, get the big promotion, and stay at that company long-term. That would have been the typical thing for someone of my generation in my industry to do. But that wasn't my path.

I decided to leave my first company about seven and a half years into my career. I was at least a year or two away from being considered for the promotion to partner. A confluence of events led to my departure, not the least of which was the existential crisis I described at the start of this chapter. That crisis was brought on, in large part, by my father's illness. A few years earlier he had been diagnosed with leukemia. Though his prognosis was good in the near term (his was a slowly progressing type), it caused a cataclysmic change in how I thought about my career, my life, and my future. I began to question everything, to constantly wonder if I was spending my time in the right way. My dad started the first of several rounds of chemotherapy about a year and a half before I quit my first job. The first course of treatment was a doozy: six months of chemotherapy and all the negative side effects associated with that. To say it was a rough, difficult time in my life would be a pretty massive understatement. But work was my refuge. And work a lot I did.

Burnout

Just as my dad was finishing his final month of chemotherapy (at least for the time being), my life became more hectic than ever before. I was slated to lead a project that would define my career—or end it. A major client was "investigating strategic alternatives" for its hotel division. In plain English, that meant the company wanted to sell its hotels and it was looking for a buyer. Think of it as listing your house for sale but on a *massive* scale. Over ninety hotels in more than twenty states would be the subject of the transaction. It was the deal of my lifetime. It was the kind of project that would make or break my career. Or at least that's what I thought at the time.

For the next six months, I literally lived and breathed that project. I did not take a single day off from May into August. Not a Saturday, not a Sunday, not Memorial Day, or July Fourth, or even Father's Day with a father who was battling leukemia. I cannot tell you how difficult that time period was for me because most of it is literally a blur in my memory.

I didn't have time to process all I was sacrificing with my family. I didn't have time to feel guilty. I barely had time to remember to brush my teeth. In those months of long nights, missed family events, eating nearly every meal at my desk, and the exhaustion that set in, suddenly all of those questions about whether I wanted to get the big promotion became moot. After the project was finally finished, I started looking for a new job almost immediately. I was burned out. I was exhausted physically (from the workload) and emotionally (from the stress). I needed some time off. A break. A chance to reset. A sabbatical. But as we all know, sabbaticals generally don't exist for most professions. People in the real, working world don't have such a luxury. I did the only thing I could think of: I quit.

The grass isn't always greener

I left for a position at a corporation that I thought would have a better work/life balance. In many ways, that was true. But in many other ways, it was completely false. I had a lot to learn. *A lot.* I dove in headfirst, trying to get up to speed on a new industry, a new company, and a whole new set of responsibilities and expectations. I was the only attorney at the corporation and the first one they had ever hired. It was my role to define and create. It was a very cool opportunity. But it was also *a lot* of work. And *a lot* of stress.

In time, I built a legal department of several paralegals and a junior attorney. I was the boss and the buck stopped with me, so to speak. That role turned out to be not very different from the demanding life I thought I had left behind.

Three years later, I made the jump back to a law firm. I joined a firm that had a (accurate) reputation for having a culture that was slower paced and more family-friendly than where I had previously been. It was a trade-off between money and expectation. It seemed to be the perfect fit for me. I joined as a partner (the title I had long coveted), and I began overseeing a team of junior attorneys and paralegals. I quickly found out (again) that being in charge is not an easy thing.

If you are looking for a pot of gold at the end of the rainbow, it is possible you may find it. But the pot of gold will only be a literal one (i.e., money). Life does not suddenly become less stressful, less hectic, more peaceful, and more manageable just because one's title changes. In some ways, it is quite the opposite, to be brutally honest.

As a young professional, I had only four things on which to concentrate all my work life energy: working lots of hours, learning as much as I could, doing a good job, and shooting for the next promotion. The boss's world is much broader, and I'm sorry to report that the hours and the stress do not necessarily decrease. At least for me, it all only got worse. As a senior-level person, I now had to worry (a lot . . . I mean a lot, a lot) about "business development," a topic that was never even mentioned, much less taught, in all my years of school. Developing a business plan, attracting new clients, pitching to prospective clients, increasing the volume of work for existing clients, budgeting, negotiating fee structures, staffing issues—I had *no idea* how to do any of this. And, of course, it is the senior-level person's responsibility to mentor, teach, and train the junior-level people. It is a great life. But it is not an easy life.

What is truly important to you?

During a really hectic stretch of client deadlines one summer, a time when I was working more hours a week than was probably healthy, my husband, Kirk, made an observation that put things into perfect perspective for me.

"I have to work all weekend *again*," I complained one evening, hoping for some sympathy.

"It sucks being the boss, doesn't it?" he replied.

What? Seriously? That was not the compassionate response I was hoping for. I was hoping for something more along the lines of, "I'm so sorry to hear that, you're working so hard, I'm so proud of you, you are amazing . . ." Nope. I got none of that.

Instead, in less than forty words, Kirk perfectly explained my life to me. He said: "Why do you think you make good money? It isn't because you don't work weekends. It isn't because it is easy. There is a reason they pay you what they do."

I was speechless. But he was right. It was not what I wanted or expected to hear in the moment. But it was the harsh truth that I *needed* to hear. These were very wise words from a very smart guy.

I was the point person on several projects for one of the company's biggest clients. This was the type of client and the type of projects I *wanted* to be in charge of: complex, challenging, high-profile stuff. It was the kind of work that was actually fun to me, the kind that my nerdy self could get excited about. Shouldn't I have expected to work long hours and to be under an incredible amount of pressure? Shouldn't I have assumed I might have to miss my niece's birthday party, or cancel dinner with my best friend, or even postpone a vacation? Shouldn't I have anticipated both the good and the not-so-good points of the life I had come to know so well?

Whenever a client had an "emergency" on a Friday afternoon, I had to change or cancel my weekend plans. I put the word emergency in quotation marks because, to be honest, is there ever really a real estate emergency on a Friday afternoon? I am not a brain surgeon. No one was going to die if I didn't work a particular weekend. But yet again, I would cancel my plans and spend my weekend at the office.

When a junior-level person missed a deadline, it was my responsibility to pick up the slack and finish the work. And, as luck would have it, this always seemed to happen at 8:00 p.m. on a Tuesday. When I had plans for the evening.

When someone on my team's work wasn't complete, or contained mistakes, or just wasn't up to par, it was my job to fix it. It was then my job to constructively tell the person what they didn't do properly and teach them how to do it better next time. And again, this always seemed to happen at the least convenient time.

I once postponed a weekend in Las Vegas not once, not twice, but three times, when the closing of a real estate deal was continually delayed. Did I mention this was a measly three-night getaway that constituted my only vacation that year? There are a million more examples I could share. But you get the point.

Trade-offs and consequences

There were trade-offs and consequences to the life I had chosen. If I was not okay with those, then maybe that life was not for me. I could wallow in self-pity, or I could embrace my reality. And if neither of those seemed like appealing choices, I could make a change and create a different kind of life. It was not anyone's fault but my own that I was a senior-level person at that company. In fact, there was no fault in it at all. It was a privilege. It just may not have been the privilege I wanted after all.

Think back for a moment to my mentor's cake eating contest analogy.

I think what he was saying is this: Being a young professional in any field is tough. But do you know what is even tougher? Being the boss. Do not expect it (the hours, the pressure, the client demands, and the consuming nature of your job) to be easy in the early years. And do not expect it get any easier as you climb the ranks. Expect it to get worse. Harder. More stressful.

Being the boss can be very rewarding. It can be interesting, challenging, and even fun sometimes. You get to be surrounded by really smart people (at least in my experience). You get to learn, think, and grow as a person and in your profession. The sense of accomplishment you feel when finishing a big project or closing an important deal is hard to beat. Colleagues and clients (for the most part) are good people who are decent to work with. And yes, some are total assholes. That's life. And, of course, the compensation is nice. But being in charge is not for everyone.

The hours can be very long. It gets incredibly stressful. Some days are better than others. Some days you will want to loudly complain (or cry, or yell, or all of the above). If you are in it for the prestige or the money, sooner or later you will find yourself unhappy and unfulfilled. But if you really appreciate what you have and if you love it, it is worth every bit of the sacrifice.

It starts and ends with knowing yourself

You have to know why you are doing it, whatever "it" is. You have to be sure all of the sacrifices that are expected of you are worth the rewards. You have to know what you want out of life. If that means a high-profile, high-pressure, high-prestige career, then you should go for it with everything you have. If something lower profile or with lower pay is okay with you in exchange for a more manageable life with more free time, then focus on careers or positions that will accommodate that. Work will suck every little thing out of you if you let it. It takes time to know yourself. It takes time to understand your "why." Why do you want to be the one in charge? Why do you want to be the one calling the shots? Is it because you thrive on the challenge? If so, good for you. But if it is because you are caught up in the competitive game of wanting what everyone else wants—as I was—you will find yourself overworked, overtired, and unfulfilled.

I spent the first forty years of my life aiming for whatever the thing was that everyone else wanted. I wanted the A grades. I wanted to be the one to hold my teacher's hand and lead the Halloween parade when I was in first grade. (I am not making this up; this is an actual, vivid memory of mine. The teacher's name was Mrs. Meyer, and I wore an angel costume that my mom handmade for me, complete with a halo made out of a coat hanger wrapped in gold piping that dug into my head and gave me a terrible headache the whole time. Regardless, I proudly led the parade with Mrs. Meyer at my side.) I desperately wanted to finish on the podium at every gymnastics competition. I needed to be on the Honor Roll, the Dean's List, and in the National Honor Society. I badly wanted to be the captain of my college cheerleading team. I wanted to graduate as a Phi Beta Kappa. And I had to have the job that everyone else wanted.

I did all of that. And still, as I hit my early forties, I found myself unfulfilled. Terribly unfulfilled. Wanting more. Needing something . . . else. Maybe even unhappy. I was striving for all these things, but not because they were what I really wanted. I was striving for them because I thought that was what would make me happy. Finally fulfilled and truly happy. I viewed happiness as an end state, a goal, or something to be accomplished.

I now know that happiness is not any of those things. It is a fluid state, always changing and moving. I now know I won't achieve some mythical state called happiness once I complete a series of steps and check all the boxes. Happiness is a state of *being*. It is not a thing one can achieve and put on a shelf like a trophy.

It takes a long time to learn about oneself. To *know* oneself. To know what you want and *why* you want those things. I wish I could tell you how to shortcut this process. But there is no easy answer.

I truly hope that reading my story and understanding my journey will help you realize yours. Go easy on yourself. Give yourself grace. It is okay to not want the thing that everyone else desires. It is even better to know what you want and follow that road, wherever it might take you.

KEY TAKEAWAYS

- It is easy to get caught up in the productivity culture ideals of working long hours, chasing the next promotion, and striving to be the boss. If that's what you truly want, go for it. Also know it is perfectly okay to choose another route.

- Work life does not get easier as you climb the career ladder. In many ways, it gets harder. The pressure, stress, and demands of your job will probably increase.

- Being the boss isn't everyone's dream, nor should it be. Being the boss can be great. But it comes with some significant trade-offs.

- Being happy is a state of *being*. It is not a task that can be completed or a thing that can be achieved.

- The hardest but most important task is to figure out your "why," what you truly want out of your career and your life.

3

If You Could Do Anything, What Would It Be?

What, like it's hard?

—ELLE WOODS, *LEGALLY BLONDE*

What if you had the chance to do anything you wanted . . . anything you dreamed of (career-wise)? Would you be confident enough to believe you could do it? Would you be fearless enough to try?

For me, it all started when my husband, Kirk, got one of those "too good to pass up" job offers. There was just one problem: the offer required a move to the other side of the country, far away from my clients and my career. Being equal spouses with equally important careers, we had always been committed to remaining in our Midwestern city. My career had deep roots there. I wasn't going anywhere. He, on the other hand, was the fortunate target of executive recruiters who contacted him with job opportunities from all corners of the country. He rarely returned their phone calls, let alone seriously entertained a job change. But even I had to admit this one was different. The company he worked for was being acquired. Instead of being on the "synergy list" (which is a nice way of saying the people who would lose their jobs), Kirk was offered a significant promotion, a position he thought no other company would offer to someone with his experience unless they knew his work firsthand. The only catch was it required a relocation.

A few weeks later, Kirk and his suitcase boarded an airplane from the frozen tundra of Wisconsin to the sunny beaches of Florida, to return only on occasion as a visitor. I stayed in the land of the cheese heads for many more months. I was in the midst of a months-long project for an important client of my company. Also, there was a house that needed to be packed up and sold, clients who needed to be informed, and more things to be done than I had ever imagined possible. Even the smallest things became complicated. Do you know you cannot legally take a cat across state lines—and certainly you cannot take one on an airplane—without medical records and a certification from your veterinarian? Or that moving companies will not transport your house plants, batteries, cleaning supplies, hairspray, light bulbs, or wine? Or that candles will melt in the moving truck, even in February? I didn't. I learned most of this the hard way.

For a while I remained with my company and split my time between cities. While the frequent flier status was nice, the constant travel became more than just tiring. I was never in one city enough for my clients and my coworkers. I was never in the other city enough for my family. I felt like I lived nowhere and everywhere at once. About a year and a half later (possibly sensing I was going to lose what little sanity remained), Kirk said these life-changing words to me: "You moved across the country for me. Now it's your turn to do what you want. It's up to you. Just do whatever it is you *really want* to do." Be careful what you wish for, people, because you just might get it.

My slightly crazy plan

I could have stayed near my comfort zone. I could have found a job exactly like my old one, just in a different city. Or I could take a chance and do something completely different. I chose the latter. I just had to figure out what it was that I really wanted to do.

Realizing I was woefully unqualified to be the Secretary General of the United Nations, I needed another plan. Saving the world seemed a bit nebulous and out of reach. And Savannah Guthrie has the market cornered on super-smart attorneys who debate important issues in front of a national audience while dressed in Prada. All of my best ideas were taken.

Law professor, I thought. I should be a law professor. I could spend my days buried in books (which, while it may sound like the first circle of hell in Dante's *Inferno* to some, is pure bliss to me). I could be surrounded by incredibly smart colleagues. I could help shape the minds of optimistic young people who want to save—or conquer—the world. I loved school from the first day of kindergarten through my last law school exam. So why not spend the rest of my career immersed in the academic world? I had finally figured it out. I had a plan.

There was just one *tiny* problem with my plan: Becoming a law professor is incredibly hard. I do not mean "incredibly hard" in that it is a tough job to land. I mean "incredibly hard" in that I might as well have said I want to be an Olympic athlete. Allow me to explain. There are roughly two hundred accredited law schools in the United States. In a given year, a particular law school may hire one or two tenure-track professors.[1] Or it may hire none. In 2014 (the year in which I joined the tenure-track ranks) only seventy-three people were hired into tenure-track positions nationwide.[2] You read that correctly. Only seventy-three people won the law school hiring game that year. Those seventy-three people became faculty members at an aggregate forty-nine law schools. What about the other 151 law schools, you ask? Collectively, they did not hire a single person.

Of the seventy-three new law professors nationwide, a whopping thirty-one of them were graduates of Harvard Law School or Yale Law School.[3] You read that correctly: Harvard and Yale graduates comprised nearly half of all new hires nationwide that year. An additional fourteen were graduates of Columbia Law School or New York University School of Law. Which is to say, graduates of just these four schools comprised forty-five of the seventy-three people hired as new law professors in the entire country that year. The remaining twenty-eight were selected from among graduates of the other 196 law schools. I was one of the lucky twenty-eight.

Had I known any of this at the time, I would have assumed I had *zero* chance of becoming a law professor. I would never have even considered submitting my resume. While I had graduated from a well-respected law school, even I admit the University of Wisconsin is not Harvard, at least not in the eyes of the academic elite. I had zero teaching experience. And I had over a dozen years of "real world" experience (which, in the academic world, is actually viewed as a negative). To make matters worse, I only sent my resume to the one law school within driving distance of my new home. At best, I did not meet the majority of the traditional hiring criteria. At worst, I was pathetically unqualified. Ignorance is bliss, though.

You won't know unless you try

In case you hadn't gleaned this already, I got the job. How did that happen? It certainly wasn't because I was the perfect candidate on paper. Not even close. It wasn't because I graduated from the "right" law school. It wasn't because I met all—or even most—of the hiring criteria. Maybe it was just dumb luck. Maybe I was in the right place at the right time. Or maybe my personality is just that dazzling. I don't know. Whatever the reason is or is not, there is one thing I know for certain: it never would have happened had I not taken a chance.

In the past I had only pursued positions for which I met (or exceeded) *all* of the qualifications. This time, though, I took a big risk. By the time I was called for an interview, my ignorant bliss had worn off and I fully realized the slim chances of getting hired. I went to the interview anyway. I interviewed for a position for which I was vastly underqualified and for which I had no directly relevant experience. I was willing to risk the possibility they would laugh in my face. I was willing to risk the thing I feared above all else: failure. There are a million reasons why I should have failed in the quest for my dream job. But I landed it.

Why should you care about my story? Why does any of this matter? You should care because it is not just *my* story. It is the story of so many women I know and millions more whom I will never meet. It is the story of how women, categorically, undersell themselves and their abilities. It is the story of how women tend to seek perfectionism and let the fear of failure direct their career decisions. It is the story of how women are conditioned to conform to traditional gender roles and expectations. Most importantly, it is the story of how women are raised, taught, conditioned, and trained not to be bold career-seekers. And it is the story of how we can begin to change our lives by changing a few beliefs within ourselves.

Men versus women: what the data tells us

Various studies have found that women apply for positions only when they meet 100 percent of the hiring criteria. In contrast, those same studies have found that men apply for positions when they meet just 60 percent of the hiring criteria.[4]

Why is that? Why do women apply for positions only when they are perfectly (or overly) qualified, whereas men apply when they barely exceed half of the hiring criteria? What is it about gender that results in this gigantic difference?

I could have easily been among those statistics. In the past, I only pursued career opportunities for which I met *all* of the qualifications. I never would have even considered submitting my resume for a position for which I met only 60 percent of the hiring criteria. Yet men do it every day.

Does this sound familiar to you? Does this sound like you? Does this sound like your friend, your spouse, or a family member of yours? What is it that women are doing differently in their professional lives than men? Are these differences hampering our career growth? And what can we women glean from men's actions that will help us propel our careers forward and upward?

(As a side note, I fully recognize the terms "men" and "women" are not inclusive of all people, that gender is not binary, that stereotypes are inherently dangerous, and that categorizing people into just two groups is inherently flawed. I use the terms because that is what the data is based upon and, in general, the trends demonstrated by the data fall along traditional gender normative lines. Even in flawed generalizations, there are resounding truths to be found. Now back to our story.)

Just one example

In the early years of our marriage, Kirk and I were singularly focused on building our respective careers: me, as an attorney at an Am Law 100 firm; he, in the finance field at a Fortune 500 company. As you probably gleaned from the stories above, my approach was to work incredibly hard, do everything right, follow every rule, keep my head down, and wait until the firm realized my brilliance and made me a partner. To say Kirk's approach was vastly different would be a major understatement.

Kirk took charge of his career in a way that never would have even occurred to me. As a young professional just out of college, he didn't wait for his genius to be noticed. He didn't wait to be plucked from the obscurity of the cubicles. He took action. He was not afraid to seek guidance from the senior executives. He found a mentor in his boss's boss. Together they charted out a path for Kirk's career and, over time, they made it happen. Kirk proactively asked to be put on more challenging projects. He spoke up, confidently. He volunteered for things that were beyond his level of expertise and experience. He let people know he was hungry for success. He studied what he did not know, and he constantly reached beyond his comfort zone. He did everything I never did to proactively assure his rise in the corporate world.

Most importantly, Kirk took risks in his career that I *never* would have taken. A decade into his career, he declined a big promotion at the Fortune 500 company where he worked to accept a similar position at a much smaller, lesser-known company, and for less money. This wasn't a situation where he was gambling on a start-up. The smaller company had existed for decades and did not appear to be particularly cutting-edge or high-growth. At the time, I told him I did not see the wisdom of leaving a company he loved, where he was well established, where his future was all but certain, on the hope that the new company might provide a better reward for the risk in the long term. I thought he was making a big mistake. I actually told him that. But I also said it was his career, and it was his choice to make. Against my brilliant advice, he accepted the offer at the smaller company for less money. I now readily admit he was right.

A few years later, he did it again. He took another big risk on the promise that a new position—one that required us to upend our entire lives—would be better for his career long-term. And so, we left the city we knew, the lives we knew, our families and friends, my company and my career, and we moved across the country for him to begin again. And, again, he was right.

Had Kirk not been willing to take two significant risks in his career (neither of which I would have done, or really even considered), he would not be where he is today. He would not have risen to become the chief financial officer of a publicly traded company at a relatively young age, and later be named president of that company. I see it so clearly now. Kirk took charge of his career. He took chances. He did not wait for things to happen *to* him; he made things happen *for himself*. He never let the fear of failure hold him back. He took risks I never would have taken. And his success today is, in part, due to that.

Find your inner Elle Woods

It is at this point in the chapter when most (male) writers would insert some sports-related quote. It would likely be something about how you miss 100 percent of the shots you never take, or how you need to skate to where the puck is going and not where the puck has been, or how it's not about whether you get knocked down but whether you get back up. You get the idea. I choose a different example. I choose Elle Woods.

Be like Elle Woods. That is the best advice I have.

I imagine this makes no sense if you haven't seen the movie *Legally Blonde*. If that's the case, then cue up Netflix, watch it, and meet me back here afterward. For those who have seen the film, please read on.

You could look at *Legally Blonde* as a meaningless, fluffy movie about a pretty sorority girl who surprises herself with success. Or, alternatively, you could see it as a social commentary on how women are viewed in the professional world and how those views impact what we believe about ourselves. You could look at it as a documentary on how women are raised, educated, treated, and conditioned to believe they aren't smart enough, they aren't good enough, they aren't tough enough, and they shouldn't even try. And you could look at it as a lesson in how women, when they believe in themselves and are willing to take risks, can be successful beyond their wildest expectations.

Here is my advice to you: strive to live every day like Elle Woods did after Warner told her she was not smart enough for law school. He viewed Elle as a hot girl in a swimsuit, one who belonged in a homecoming parade but not in a courtroom. Live to prove him wrong. Show him you can be both. Be stubborn. Raise your hand. Speak up. Buy a new laptop while wearing your bunny costume. Don't be intimidated by those who think they are smarter than you (because they probably aren't). Don't merely settle for what is expected of you. Do not let the views of your parents, your friends, or your boyfriend hold you back. Apply to Harvard anyway. Prove them wrong. Push yourself to work harder and achieve more. Be determined. Be ambitious. Believe in yourself and take chances, just as Elle did.

Believe in yourself even when others doubt you. Believe in yourself *especially* when others doubt you. Do whatever you have to do to prove them wrong. When you're tired and you want to give up, let their words of doubt fuel your fire. Do not let others' perceptions of you dictate your self-worth. Take a chance, even if you aren't entirely sure of what to do next. Do not let others' opinions of you shape *your* future.

Be bold. Take risks. Do not be afraid of failure. Go for the job you want, even if you are not quite qualified. Go for that internship with Professor Callahan even though you know he is only going to pick the four brightest students in the entire class.

Have the confidence to know you can do it. Bluff a little if you must. You may not have the highest IQ score in the room—but you have other strengths. Find your strengths and use them to your advantage. Elle didn't know how to cross-examine a witness. She didn't know the law very well. She had zero courtroom experience to draw upon. But she did know Prada shoes. And hair care. And wet T-shirt contests. And that knowledge made all the difference.

Most importantly, be true to yourself, just as Elle Woods was true to herself. She didn't change her pink clothes, her bouncy blonde hair, her bubbly personality, her love of fashion, or her manicured nails to try to fit in at Harvard Law. Instead, she tapped into the best version of herself, used what she knew best, and she succeeded. You can too.

And for those of you who are wondering, when I submitted my resume to the law school, I did not put it on pink paper. But I wanted to.

KEY TAKEAWAYS

- Be like Elle Woods. That is the best advice I can give.
- Be bold. Take risks. Take a chance. Go after the job you want even if you aren't qualified for it. You just might surprise yourself.
- Do not settle for what society expects of you. Dream bigger.
- Believe in yourself even when others doubt you. Live to prove them wrong.
- Find your unique strengths and use them to your advantage.
- Always, always be true to who you are.

4

There Is No Such Thing as "Having It All"

You can't have it all at once. Over my lifespan, I think I have had it all. But in different periods of time, things were rough.

**—RUTH BADER GINSBURG,
UNITED STATES SUPREME COURT JUSTICE**

E very day, we are bombarded with images and messages of perfect people living perfect lives. Yes, I am talking about social media. But I'm also talking about so much more than that. Even before the days of Instagram, women of my generation were constantly being told they can be perfect, they can "have it all," and they should strive for that. The influencers of my generation were more analog—magazine ads, television commercials, movies, books, and the daily culture that surrounded us—but the message was the same as it is today: Women can (and should) be perfect. And if you are not perfect, there must be something wrong with you that you can, and should, try to fix. There's a face cream for this, a new workout regime for that, an app to make you more productive, and a new gadget for you to fix your life. You need to be a girl boss and have a side hustle, too. Oh, and don't forget to get enough sleep and spend ample amounts of time on self-care. You need those, too. Not to mention, you need to fix your parenting and perfect your relationships . . . honestly, it is *exhausting*.

I'm here to tell you that perfection does not exist. "Having it all" is just a figment of some 1980s imagination. Even people whose lives seem perfect are, in actuality, far from it. We all struggle. We all have our shit to deal with. You just don't see it.

Perfect from the outside

I have a few girlfriends whose lives look idyllic from the outside. Yes, they have great privilege. Yes, they have it easy compared to most of the world. They were lucky enough to be born into families where basic needs were not only met but exceeded. They had parents (or at least one parent) who loved and cared for them. They had the privileges of attending good schools, living in safe places, and having what they needed to be healthy and happy. They had the opportunity and financial means to go to college.

Today, they have great careers, healthy kids, ample resources, and even some extra money to take vacations now and then. They are smart, pretty, athletic, and accomplished. In our young and single days, they had plenty of guys chasing them. Things just seemed to come *easy* for them.

They are the lucky ones. Their lives look pretty damn perfect from the outside. And even they are struggling. Sometimes a lot.

That's the point of this story: Even seemingly perfect people are far from it. Let me pull back the curtain and show you the reality of my "perfect" friends, and maybe then we can all exhale and stop striving for some unattainable state of being. Maybe then we can recognize that life is hard. For everyone. Even for the most privileged and gifted among us. So please, let me introduce you to a few of my perfectly imperfect friends.

The Stanford friend

I was just nine months into my career when I met Karrie, my Stanford friend.

But before I tell you about her, a little background. I had interned at a law firm during the summer after my second year of law school and joined full time after graduation. The firm was (and still is) the largest and most prestigious one in my home state, with additional offices spanning the country from New York to Miami to Houston to Los Angeles. The firm hires mostly from Ivy League schools and other top programs. At my school, the University of Wisconsin, scoring a job offer from this particular place is THE job to get. Sure, there are firms headquartered in New York and Los Angeles that are larger and arguably more prestigious on a national level. But in America's Dairyland, Foley & Lardner is the shit.

I met Karrie when I was a "first year," meaning a junior person with less than one year of experience. Shortly before the arrival of the summer interns that June, I started hearing some buzz about one of the students who would be joining us for the summer. No one usually cared much about an individual student. No one person typically stood out from the crowd. The buzz was particularly perplexing because the student I was hearing about was a "1L," meaning she had only completed one year of law school thus far. Most of the thirty or so summer interns were "2Ls," meaning they had completed two years of law school. Why was Karrie the 1L the topic of conversation? Sure, she was from Stanford. But the firm had other people from Stanford (and from Harvard, Yale, Michigan, and other top schools). I am not sure Karrie was even the only Stanford student that summer. I was intrigued.

By coincidence or design, the powers that be assigned Karrie a spot in an office just two doors down from mine. On Karrie's first day, one of the partners asked me to "keep an eye out" for her. Take her out for lunch. Be nice to her. Make sure she felt comfortable. Again, I wondered why everyone was so impressed with this 1L from Stanford. Since when was the firm actually *concerned* about the impression it made on a single student? From what I could tell, no one gave much thought to pretty much any of my coworkers or me. We all felt a bit like cogs in a machine. Because we were. Because that is how large law firms operate.

Then I heard about her background and it started to make some sense. She had earned a near-perfect score on the LSAT (the law school admissions test). She had near-perfect grades. At *Stanford*, one of the most difficult schools in the country to get into. She was a local kid, meaning the firm had a good chance of convincing her to return to Wisconsin long-term. Probably unfairly, I assumed she would be a real dud. I assumed she would be a book-smart nerd with zero personality. I assumed she would be the kind of curve-breaker who could ace an exam but couldn't carry on a conversation at a cocktail party. I was waiting for her to stare at her feet with her unkept hair in her face, hiding behind glasses and mismatched, out-of-fashion clothes. I mean, she's a superstar at Stanford, where the smartest of the smart people are. She couldn't possibly have had time to pay attention to fashion, conversation, or how she looked on a daily basis. Right?

Wrong. I could not have been more wrong. I don't know what struck me more when I first met her: Her gigantic, warm smile or her big, bouncy, blonde hair. She was like a walking, talking beauty pageant winner with the brain of a genius and the charm of a talk show host. She can't be real, I thought.

Luckily for me, for the firm, and for everyone who knows her, Karrie is very real. To meet her is to feel immediately at ease. Her laugh can travel across a football field. Her work ethic—let's just say she works as hard as anyone I have ever known. All that plus a genius-level brain equals one very powerful package. She returned to the firm the following summer and, eventually, after graduation.

By the time Karrie finished school and joined the firm full time, I was a "fourth year," and I was moving up in the world. No longer a newbie, I was experienced enough to be trusted with clients and handle much of my work without someone overseeing me. As a new hire, Karrie was working under a more senior person whose primary client was a major player in the media industry. That client was on an acquisition spree for a few years, meaning we were almost always working on a deal to buy more media outlets. I handled the real estate, and the partner (with Karrie's help) handled the corporate end. Within a year, it was just twenty-five-year-old Karrie and twenty-nine-year-old me handling this client's work. We thought we were pretty cool: two young female attorneys facing off against men twice our age.

It's completely normal to feel overwhelmed

If Karrie and I hadn't solidified our lifelong friendship in those early years, we definitely achieved it late one night in a conference room somewhere in Chicago. We were working on the client team for a very important deal. The funny thing is I don't even remember which client, which deal, or even what year it was. I do remember the hours were grueling. We had spent evenings, weekends, and a long holiday (Memorial Day? Labor Day? Easter? Your guess is as good as mine). within the walls of our offices for months, trying to beat impossible deadlines. The culmination of those months of hard work—the actual closing of the deal—took place in some since-forgotten conference room in Chicago.

There is a certain camaraderie and trust that develops when working long hours under stressful conditions with coworkers who are your age. Call it the foxhole mentality if you want (not that I'm equating where we worked to actual war; it's just an expression).

Late into the night, I left the conference room where I was working to find Karrie. I found her in another conference room with a certain look on her face. I knew that look. She was having one of those "I can't keep doing this" moments. I knew exactly what was going on because I, too, have had those moments. But I also had a few more years of experience to know that it wouldn't always be this bad, that there would be slower times, and that life would not always feel completely out of control.

I said, "Let's go somewhere else." We found an out-of-the-way place where no one else could see or hear us. It was my duty as a friend, a colleague, and a fellow female to help her through this. The more I talked, the less it seemed to help, though.

At one point she said, "How do you keep doing this year after year?" I gave her some answer about how it will get better. She said, "No, I mean *literally* how do you do it? How do you clean your house? When do you do your laundry? How are your clothes ironed? Because none of that is getting done for me right now. I'm literally running out of clean clothes to put on." Tears rolled down her face as she asked me this.

Many of our male colleagues had stay-at-home wives who handled those things. In my house, I *am* the wife, and my husband worked at least as many hours as I did. Karrie wasn't married at the time. Neither of us had the luxury of a spouse or partner who could carry the load—or even part of it.

That is when I let Karrie in on my little (big) secret. "My mom,"

I said. She looked confused. "My mom cleans my house. She does my laundry. She irons my clothes and puts them in the closet. She waits for contractors to fix things at my house. In a pinch, she'll do my grocery shopping, pick up my dry-cleaning, and whatever else I need. Kirk and I couldn't do what we do without her help." That was the raw, brutal, truth. As a thirty-year-old professional woman, I literally could not have functioned as an adult with the career I had without the constant help of my mom.

"Do you think your mom would do that for me?" Karrie asked. I don't know, but I'll find out, I told her. That's how my mom became the indispensable helper and surrogate mom to Karrie and later, also to our friend Jenna, another coworker who was struggling to keep up with the constant chores of adult life due to her all-consuming career.

You don't have to do everything yourself

What is the lesson learned here? Maybe it is that demanding jobs are not conducive to a normal life. But I don't accept that. There are ways to make it work.

Maybe the lesson is that the burden unfairly falls on women, even when the woman is the primary income-earner, and we need to find ways to reallocate that burden. If you have a spouse or partner, don't assume you have to do everything—or even most things—yourself. Ask for help. Demand help, if you must. Tell them what you need. Share the burden. I spent way too many years silently and resentfully handling the bulk of the household chores and life obligations (i.e., buying all of the Christmas presents, sending all of the birthday cards, etc.). It did not have to be that way. My husband was blissfully unaware of my struggle. Once I finally clued him in, he was happy to take some of the load. To this day, he does his own laundry and irons his own clothes. And I handle mine. We trade off on doing the grocery shopping. If one person cooks dinner, the other does the dishes. It isn't completely equal, but it's a hell of a lot closer to equal than not.

If you have a partner and you feel like you are doing most of the domestic chores and life duties, please don't keep doing that. This is such a critically important topic. I can't even begin to do it justice within the pages of this book. If this resonates with you at all, I beg you to pull up your Amazon app right now, type "Eve Rodsky Fair Play" into the search bar, and order her book.[1] A while back, a good friend of mine recommended this book to me. And I, in turn, now recommend it to pretty much every woman I know. It can change your life, or at least change your thoughts about your life. If reading isn't your thing, there is also a documentary called *Fair Play*, based on Eve Rodsky's book, which you can find on Apple TV+, Prime Video, and other streaming services.[2] I also religiously follow Eve Rodsky and her Fair Play movement on Instagram for daily tips and hints for creating a more equitable life for everyone in my family.

Maybe the lesson is that it takes a village. Maybe you don't have a spouse or partner, or maybe the two of you are both busy and can't handle it all yourselves (as Kirk and I were). We needed my mom, a lot, even at the age of thirty. Let your village help you. If you don't have a village, maybe you are fortunate enough to be in a position where you can hire one. I realize not everyone has that luxury. Housecleaning, lawn cutting, grocery shopping, and what-ever else you can outsource—if you have the financial means, do it. Save your precious time for what really matters: for your family and yourself. I can pay Instacart to do my grocery shopping and deliver it to my door, but I can't hire someone to negotiate a contract for my client. I can pay the dry-cleaner to press my clothes, but I can't hire someone to take an ill parent or child to the doctor. I can pay a lawn service to cut the grass and weed the flower beds, but I am the only one who can spend my wedding anniversary with my husband. You get the idea.

If you are fortunate enough to be in the financial position to take some of the burden off yourself, please do it. You will be a happier, more productive, less resentful, and less stressed human being. I promise. It won't take away the unreasonable hours your career will sometimes demand, and it isn't a solution for the sad-but-true reality that women shoulder more of the household burden than men, regardless of income or career. But it is at least a way to help keep your sanity and maintain your health. Do what you need to do to protect and preserve yourself. That is the lesson Karrie, Jenna, and I learned and fully embraced.

If you aren't in a financial position to outsource any chores and tasks, maybe you can find other means of support. Maybe you have family members who can take a little bit of the burden off of you—parents, siblings, or even close friends or neighbors. If you have children who are old enough, enlist their help. Not only will it alleviate some of the burden on you, but it will also teach them good life skills. Wouldn't it be great if every eighteen-year-old arrived at college or her first apartment knowing how to do laundry, plan meals, budget for groceries, cook, clean, take the dog to the veterinarian, shop for Christmas gifts, and so on?

If none of those are options for you, check in with your circle of friends. There are people who love you and support you (emotionally); maybe they have even a sliver of time to help in some way. When my friend Nicole returned to work after giving birth to twins, she struggled mightily just to get enough sleep, do her job, and keep two tiny humans alive and well. She and her husband didn't have the financial resources to outsource chores or hire someone to help, and they didn't have family who could pitch in. That's when she turned to her circle of friends. They were all working moms, too, none of whom had much time. But they found ways to help each other. On Sunday afternoons when one friend made dinner for her own family, she made a second batch for Nicole. It wasn't much more work for her, and it saved Nicole from making one night's dinner each week. Another came to Nicole's house for one hour each weekend just to fold baskets filled with clean, tiny baby clothing. In return, Nicole found ways to help them too. Together they found ways—ways that didn't cost anyone any money—to help one another. It takes a village, after all.

The grocery store incident

Now back to our story about my seemingly perfect friend Karrie.

Today, Karrie is a forty-something mom with three school-aged children. She is a classroom mom, the chairperson of a nonprofit board, and an incredible friend. She also happens to be a majorly important person at a prestigious international law firm. She rose through the ranks from associate to partner in record time despite having had three babies along the way. She's held the additional positions of hiring partner and chair of her department. And someday, I expect she will be running the place.

Even though she is one of my very close friends, and even though I know her schedule intimately, I literally do not understand when she has time to sleep. In lawyerly terms, she's a rainmaker. In mom terms, she's the head of the PTA. In people terms, she's amazing. I share this with you not to brag about my incredible friend (although that's easy to do). I share this to demonstrate that even the most seemingly perfect people struggle just like the rest of us.

One of my favorite stories about Karrie dates back several years, to when her oldest child was in kindergarten, the baby was just a baby, and there was one more kid in between those two. After picking up the oldest from school and a quick stop at day care to grab the toddler and the baby, Karrie realized there was nothing in her kitchen to make for dinner. She hadn't planned on needing to pick up all three kids *and* figure out dinner. She and her husband usually use the "divide and conquer" method of parenting and running a household. But with him unexpectedly delayed at some airport somewhere, she knew she would be the only available parent that night.

While overworked adults can survive for periods of time on Uber Eats deliveries or whatever we can conjure up from the refrigerator, tiny humans need to eat a decent dinner. Karrie knew this. Karrie needed to stop at the grocery store. Grocery shopping with one child is challenging enough; shopping with three kids is utter chaos. But a girl has to do what a girl has to do. At least it wasn't wintertime, she thought. Hauling three kids and a grocery cart through a snowy parking lot would have been *too much* to handle at that moment. Karrie grabbed the grocery cart, placed the toddler in the seat facing her, put the baby's carrier in the basket of the cart, and took the oldest child's hand. Pushing two kids in a grocery cart with one hand reminded her she needed to get back to the gym. Someday. When she has more time. Maybe when the kids finish high school.

With two children in the cart, there was precious little room for the actual groceries. You know, the things she needed to buy so she could take them home and make something to feed the tiny people. After filling all available space in the cart, Karrie surveyed her options. She could go home without everything she needed, she could clone herself, or she could figure out a way to get it done. She chose the latter. She grabbed a box of cereal and told the toddler to hold it on his lap. Then she grabbed a loaf of bread. A loaf of bread doesn't weigh much, she figured. She carefully placed the loaf of bread on top of the baby in his carrier. She then placed a few cans of soup beside the baby in his carrier. With her oldest child helping to fetch items off the shelves and carefully balancing them in the cart, Karrie was feeling pretty good about herself. She was ready to declare victory. She paused for a moment when her oldest child asked her, "Mama, is *this* too heavy to stack on the baby?" A few hot dog buns can't be too heavy, she reasoned. A box of taco shells is pretty light, too.

So went the rest of the shopping trip, with her oldest child repeatedly asking, "Mama, is THIS too heavy to stack on the baby? Is THAT too heavy to stack on the baby?" The scene raised some eyebrows among the perfectly accessorized yoga moms who seem to have endless amounts of time to look glamorous, even at the grocery store. But for the rest of us, this is our reality. Even for the very successful, highly accomplished, genius-level women among us, this is real life. There are times when we just have to stack the bread on the baby and get the shopping done!

When Karrie told me this story, she was not telling it to entertain a crowd at a cocktail party. She was not trying to be funny (although the visual is pretty funny in hindsight). She was telling a vulnerable story about just one struggle of just one day. She was being real, true, and blatantly honest. Karrie was telling a close friend that her life—a life that looks pretty idyllic from the outside—is far from easy.

Life is hard. Life with children is even harder. Life with children and a demanding career can seem damn-near impossible at times. We all feel that way. That is the thing that I want everyone to understand. No matter how easy someone's life may seem from the outside, they fight battles we know nothing about. They struggle just like the rest of us. They need help with their laundry, their grocery shopping, and a million other things. They cut corners at times. They run out of clean socks like the rest of us. And yes, sometimes they stack bread on the baby.

Some days the victory will be just making it through the day. And that's enough.

Life is hard for everyone

Gabi and I met in the first week of the first month of our first year of college. She was the girl in front of me as I walked into the gym on tryout day for the college cheerleading team. It was hard to miss the bouncy blonde ponytail wrapped in a bright pink bow (which, of course, perfectly matched her bright pink shorts and bright pink lipstick). Her eyes were as blue, wide, and innocent as your favorite Snapchat filter, except Snapchat would not be invented for another fifteen years.

She was perfect, I thought, all 5 feet and less than 115 pounds of her. In case you are wondering, I know she weighed less than 115 pounds because the female cheerleaders had a 120-pound weight limit, and Gabi was on the small side of all the girls on the team. (Which is a misogynistic and disturbing topic for another day, for there is no better way to inflict emotional distress and disordered eating upon young women than to impose a weight limit on them. But as I said, I'll leave that topic for another time. Now back to our story.)

"There's this cheerleader," guys would say to me repeatedly for the next four years. Yes, I know who you are talking about. Her name is Gabi, and yes, she has a boyfriend. I said these words so many times that I had the response ready to go even before the guy finished asking the question.

Even my own mother referred to Gabi as "The Beautiful One." My mom loved to tell people her daughter was one of the cheerleaders. When they'd ask which one, she'd say, "The one with red hair." (In my mom's defense, my college cheerleading team consisted of eight guys, seven girls with blonde hair, and me. I didn't look like Merida from the movie *Brave* or anything close to that, but my hair was definitely different than the others.) She would follow that up by saying, "The Beautiful One is my daughter's friend," while pointing down at the basketball court where Gabi was standing. To this day, my mom still refers to Gabi that way. I recently said I was meeting a friend for dinner. Her response? "Oh, is it the really beautiful one?" At least that time she added in the word "really" for some variety.

Despite everything I just said, I've never, ever been jealous of Gabi. She is the kind of girl whom other girls would hate, if only they could. But that just is not possible. Gabi's incredibly sweet and genuine self doesn't allow any room for jealousy or hatred. To know her is to love her. She has zero ego. She has the biggest heart. She loves with every ounce of her being. She cares genuinely and feels deeply. She appreciates every gift she has been given and she takes nothing for granted. Best of all, she sees the good in everyone.

Not the worst mother in the world

Years ago, I met Gabi for lunch one Friday as we often did when we lived in the same city. This is how our lunch dates usually went: between quick replies to clients via text, we talked at rapid speed to catch up on each other's lives while simultaneously shoving food into our mouths as fast as we could, all in a rush to get back to the office before another crisis could erupt.

Sometime during that lunch, like nearly every lunch before it that year, Gabi uttered the dreaded words. "I am the worst mother in the world," she said. "No, you aren't," I replied, as I always did.

Gabi was doing her best to keep all the balls in the air in those years. She was working a high-profile job as a marketing executive at a major company. She had two children under the age of five. Like every young family I know, Gabi and her husband were struggling to juggle raising children, navigating demanding careers, and maintaining their own relationship, as well as those with family, friends, and themselves. Like every working mom I know, Gabi thought she was the worst mother in the world at times. And, with her close friends, she sometimes admitted that out loud. It was usually followed by some tears. I made it my job as her friend to tell her often and always, "No, you are not." Sometimes what followed that sentence was just plain *funny* (at least in hindsight). This was one of those times.

The prior Sunday night, Gabi noticed a flyer on the kitchen table from the preschool her children attended. The preschool was always sending home these types of flyers and filling her inbox with emails she did not have time to read. Most of the flyers and emails were unimportant; they usually discussed upcoming cupcake days and other trivial things she did not have time for. In any given day, her inbox would be filled with messages from ten other moms discussing who was bringing what snack to which playdate that weekend. Gabi didn't have time to get lost in the weeds of the stay-at-home parent email extravaganza. She mostly just minded her own business when it came to the mom groups.

This particular flyer, though, laid out the themes for the upcoming "Crazy Week." She must have missed that email. And the five other reminder emails. The very next day, Monday, was "crazy sock day." Great, she thought. It was Sunday night, after bedtime, and she needed to come up with crazy socks in the next eight hours. Gabi improvised. She found the most colorful non-matching socks in her husband's drawer and laid them out for her son to wear. When Gabi picked up her son on Monday afternoon and asked about crazy sock day, her son replied with a lackluster, "It was fine." She chalked it up to him being a shy little boy. Tuesday was "crazy hair day." Gabi set her alarm early so she would have time to do something, well, crazy with her son's very short hair. Tuesday evening her son was equally blasé in response to Gabi's inquiries. Wednesday was "pajama day." Gabi dressed her son in his favorite pajamas that morning. While time has diminished my ability to remember the exact details, I recall the pajamas being something in the superhero genre.

Gabi was in the middle of another typical busy day at the office when she received a call from her son's teacher. The preschool didn't call unless there was a decent-to-good reason to get in touch with a parent during the workday. Most things could wait until pickup time. Her son was feeling fine that morning so it couldn't be that he was sick, she thought. Maybe he got hurt somehow? What else could be wrong? The teacher informed Gabi that her son was upset, crying, and wanted to go home. What was wrong? The teacher quietly said, "Do you know your son came to school today in his *pajamas?*" Of course he came to school in his pajamas. It's pajama day. Right?

Oh no. Oh no. Oh shit.

Please, please don't let this be true, Gabi thought. She closed her eyes for a brief moment to let it all sink in. It was like time stood still while she processed the events of the last three days.

It immediately dawned on Gabi what had happened. She had sent the *wrong child* to school in pajamas. It must have been her two-year-old daughter's teacher, not her four-year-old son's teacher, who sent home the "Crazy Week" flyer. They attended the same preschool. All the flyers looked alike. She assumed it was her son's class because, well, it didn't make a lot of sense to have "Crazy Week" for kids in diapers who didn't understand what was happening around them. It was only logical to conclude you'd do crazy socks and crazy hair with a four-year-old, not a toddler with very little hair to begin with.

That's right, readers. Sometimes we are so busy that we send the wrong kid to school in his pajamas. Sometimes we are so busy that we don't read every word of every fluffy preschool flyer. We focus in on the critical information, and we execute. Wednesday. Pajamas. Done.

The lesson for us all

Why am I bothering to tell this story? What does this have to do with the role of women in the workplace or how we can harness our talents to achieve greater success?

I am telling this story because it is important for us all to realize that even people whose lives seem pretty charmed—people with great careers, beautiful faces, a head full of brains, great spouses or partners, and generally happy lives—even those people struggle under all of the competing demands on their time. Even those people feel like a total failure sometimes.

As much as people have fawned over Gabi for much of her life, the real truth is that Gabi isn't perfect. She isn't infallible. She has the same insecurities and self-doubts as the rest of us. Outward beauty does not stop the self-questioning and uncertainty we all face simply because we are human. Maybe that is the lesson I want you to learn from this wonderful creature who is my dear friend.

Someone's life might look easy from the outside. Someone might appear to "have it all." She might be beautiful, and desirable, and the object of affection. She might also be talented, hard-working, and really smart, like Gabi is. She might have won awards, given keynote talks, and achieved great things, like Gabi has. Things might seem to come easy to her. Her life might seem easy from an outsider's perspective. You might envy that person or be jealous of all she has. But her life is not without stress, problems, mistakes, or the occasional feeling of being a total failure. We are all merely human.

The truth is we all have problems. We all have insecurities. We all have things we aren't good at, and things we wish we could change. We all get overstressed, overworked, and overwhelmed at times. We all make mistakes. No one's life is perfect. Life is not easy. For anyone. Not even for The Beautiful One.

Life does not pause for work

Life is messy. And sometimes that messy life means work gets in the way of even the most personal of things. Sometimes people who've accomplished great things still struggle with the most fundamental and private of life's tasks.

What follows isn't glamourous or worthy of bragging about. But it is real. It is unfiltered and honest. And it's a great reminder that life does not pause for you just because you have too much work to do. Yes, the work has to get done. Yes, our schedules are crazy at times, so crazy that we sometimes do not have time for the most basic of tasks. And yes, personal things—things that no one else can really do for us—need to be taken care of. It is our burden to figure out how to handle all of this . . . somehow, in the best way we can.

The breast pump incidents

During our early working years, my good friend Anna and I watched as most of our female friends left promising careers shortly after having their first babies. It seemed like an inevitable, vicious cycle: graduate near the top of the class from a well-respected university, land a great job at a prestigious company, dedicate your twenty-something years to your career, get married, have a baby, return from maternity leave (exhausted), give every ounce of your being to try to continue your career while not completely failing at keeping an infant fed and clothed, then sooner or later (usually sooner) realize you simply cannot continue. Cue the submission of the resignation letter, usually within a handful of months of said baby's arrival. We watched this cycle repeat again and again. And again. To too many of our female coworkers.

Anna was determined to defy the odds. She was determined to stop the cycle before its final stage. She was not willing to give up on her career or her desire to have children. She decided to take on the seemingly impossible challenge of having a baby, then another, then another, all while continuing to progress in her career.

After a typical maternity leave, Anna returned to work while still breastfeeding her first baby. Necessarily, then, there were times at which Anna needed to utilize the modern wonder of the breast pump. For those who are unfamiliar with this piece of wizardry, please use your imagination. The milk needs to get from inside the body to outside the body and into a bottle. There is a mechanism, called a breast pump, that one uses to accomplish this task.

At the time, Anna's company did not have a dedicated room for nursing moms. There was no lactation suite, no lounge with a locking door, and no other place for anyone in need of privacy or rest. To complicate matters, Anna's company did not allow locking doors on offices. During the first few months after her return to work, Anna was forced to "pump" (yes, this is a verb in the parenting vernacular) while sitting idly in a bathroom stall. This, of course, is unacceptable today, at least in the view of most people. But it was not at all unusual fifteen years ago. Some business environments still lack a dedicated space for nursing moms or anyone else in need of a little privacy.

After a few weeks of sitting in a bathroom stall with her breast pump, Anna finally convinced the company she needed a lock on her office door. She was fortunate to be in a role where she had a private office. Many women at her company worked in cubicles or in an open-office environment. They had no option for a locking door. Anna was one of the lucky ones. She would now be able to pump, when needed, from the privacy of her office. This, of course, would also allow her to get her work done while pumping. Let the multi-tasking begin, she thought. Anna was ready to declare victory for all nursing moms, or at least those who were senior enough to have the privilege of a private office. That is, until a few glitches arose. The first glitch occurred while Anna was on a conference call with a client. When she needed to pump, she momentarily put the call on mute, locked her office door, and set up the pump. The call continued uneventfully for a short while. This is going great, she thought. Then, when Anna was speaking (and the mute button was unengaged), the client said, "There's that strange noise again." Oh no, Anna thought. "It sounds like a swooshing noise," the client said. That's right. Anna's client could hear the pump doing its job. She couldn't turn it off because then the client would know the noise was coming from her end. She finished the call, turned off the pump, and vowed to only use it from then on when she was not on a phone call. Problem solved.

The second glitch can be summed up in two words: window washers. I can attest that, when one works in a high-rise office building with no adjacent buildings immediately facing yours, one feels a sense of privacy despite the floor-to-ceiling windows. That is, until one comes face-to-glass-to-face with the window washers. Unfortunately for Anna, that year the window washers found the most inopportune time to reach her floor. Anna was sitting at her desk, working and pumping. Then she heard the noise outside her window. She looked up to find the window washers staring back at her. She furiously scrambled to find something to cover herself. The window washers furiously scrambled to move to the next office. Who EVER would have thought about the window washers?

Anna is one of the lucky ones. She had a great job and resources at her disposal. She had the advantage of being in a senior-level role with a private office. Her status in the company made it easier for her to insist on accommodations (even though she should not have had to). And even she couldn't escape the reality that sometimes real life, in all its messiness, gets in the way of work and sometimes work, in all its craziness, gets in the way of life.

The Walgreens incident

Unfortunately, what follows is another entirely true story. Even more unfortunately, it is about me. This dramedy dates back to when I was in my early thirties. I've told you about this time in my life already. I was leading the project team for the sale of a client's hotel division. It was a career-making (or breaking) opportunity for me. I was intimidated, overwhelmed, and even a little scared to be heading up such a big project for a big client. I knew my future at the company would depend on how I performed in this moment (or, rather, in every moment over a six-month period).

It is not a stretch to say this project took over my life for that time. I missed family dinners, birthdays, and my nieces' dance recitals. I hadn't seen my best friends in months, despite the fact that two of them lived less than ten minutes from me. I was late to virtually everything I attempted to attend, even on a Saturday night. I cancelled the appointment with my hair stylist *again* (which, I might add, is an act of small bravery for someone who dyed her hair blonde at the time). I gave up on makeup, ironing my clothes, and all but the most necessary of personal needs. I skipped at least one dentist appointment and postponed every doctor's checkup. For months, my meals came from delivery services and vending machines. I was somewhat convinced my cat was going to petition for emancipation on the grounds that I was never home.

For that entire summer and into the fall, my life could have literally been summed up in a few words: work, sleep, shower, repeat.

Before we proceed, I need to explain something to the younger generations. Before the ubiquity of online shopping and Amazon Prime deliveries, most things had to be purchased at an actual retail store. We had to get into a car, drive to the place that sold the thing we needed, go inside the building, find the thing we needed, and take it to an actual human being to pay for it. It may sound like *The Flintstones* to us now. But it was the dawn of the new millennium. And I was in need of some of those things that were only sold in stores.

For the third day in a row, I was racing to leave the office in time to reach Walgreens before the doors closed. It was becoming clear I was not going to make it . . . again. That's when my husband called me. I instantly broke into tears. "What's wrong? Why are you crying? And what can I do to help?" Kirk asked. "Nothing," I replied. I told him there are certain things I needed to take care of myself. Eventually, sensing the urgency, he insisted. Eventually, in my desperation, I relented. I told Kirk I needed to pick up a prescription at the pharmacy. And I needed tampons. You heard me correctly. Tampons. This is real life, people, and things are not always glamorous.

It seems I told Kirk the brand name of tampons I needed, but I failed to specify the size. By the time he arrived at Walgreens, I was knee deep in my work and nowhere near my phone. Staring at a shelf filled with various brands, types, and sizes of tampons, Kirk did what any great problem-solver would do. He grabbed a box in each size and proceeded to the pharmacy counter. He gave the pharmacist my name. Imagine the pharmacist's surprise at seeing my six-foot-four, thirty-three-year-old husband in his business suit standing with a basket full of tampon boxes. The pharmacist returned with the prescription. Kirk later told me the pharmacist said something along the lines of, "Wow, you're a good guy." You see, the prescription I needed was of the certain female hormone–containing variety (i.e., birth control pills). That's right, people. Sometimes we are so busy that we need a trusted someone to buy our tampons and pick up our birth control pills.

Why our stories matter

Why am I telling this humiliating story about myself? Why did I tell you all of the (true, vulnerable, and funny) stories about Karrie, Gabi, and Anna? Why am I sharing any of this? Because in this social media world, sometimes we need a loud reminder that even people whose lives appear to be under control are, in fact, struggling to keep it all together. Some days we are only one small task away from having everything come crumbling down around us.

No one is perfect.

Karrie—however wonderful and amazing she is—is not perfect. Ditto for Gabi. And Anna. And me. In fact, we are very far from perfect.

Sometimes we are late to pick up our children from day care. Sometimes we forget a friend's birthday. Or we miss a family dinner. We do a conference call at midnight from the vestibule of a casino in Las Vegas. We finish a presentation while riding a bus across three states to the next dance competition. Sometimes we postpone a vacation, then postpone it again, before finally getting on the airplane. And once we get there, we answer our boss's call while standing in a vineyard in Napa because business has to get done. Sometimes we have to cancel a client meeting because our family needs us more. Sometimes we quietly negotiate a deal from a hospital room while sitting beside our ailing parent. Some days we think we just cannot take it anymore. But other days feel perfect, and that makes it all worth it.

To the women of the next generation, please learn from us. Please do not spend the next twenty years trying to be perfect. Realize that no one is flawless, and no one has an easy life regardless of how that life may look from the outside. No one can "have it all" unless we redefine what "all" means. You cannot be the top salesperson, the parent of the year, and the ideal spouse or partner all at once. It may be that you will not ever be any of those things, and that's okay.

Realize that most of our lives are far from the filtered pictures we see on social media. Please know that "good enough" is sometimes all you will have time for, and that *is* enough. Our lives are busy and

messy and complicated. Know that, at some point, everyone runs out
of clean socks. Or tampons. Or you might send the wrong kid to
school in his pajamas. Even the most perfect among us feels like we
might lose our mind sometimes. We are all just doing the best we can in
the time we have. Any day you are here on earth, with your family and
friends, is a good day. Concentrate on who or what is truly important
to you. Stop doing what you think you *should* do. Do what makes
you happy. Stop feeling guilty about not being with your family
when you are working. Stop feeling guilty about not attending to
work matters when you are with family.

The sooner we realize that no one is perfect, and the sooner we
stop pursuing that unattainable goal of work/life balance, the better
off we will all be. We all do what we need to do to make it through
each day. And some days, that means stacking the bread on the baby.
And that's perfectly fine.

KEY TAKEAWAYS

- We are an overscheduled, overly busy, over-tasked, overcommitted society. We all need help getting things done
  sometimes. Find help where you can. If you have a spouse or
  partner, look at the division of household duties. Maybe you
  are fortunate enough to have the financial resources to outsource some things. Maybe your family or friends can help. It
  takes a village.

- Life is not easy for anyone. No matter how perfect someone's
  life may seem, or how smart or beautiful they are, or how much
  success they've gained, everyone struggles at times.

- Go easy on yourself. We are all just doing the best we can in
  the time we have.

- If you must, go ahead and stack the bread on the baby. She
  won't mind.

5

Representation Matters

Women make up more than half of the world's population and potential, so it is neither just nor practical for their voices, for our voices, to go unheard at the highest levels of decision-making.

—MEGAN MARKLE, DUCHESS OF SUSSEX

My sister Lisa is very good at a lot of things. Lisa is incredibly smart. More than a decade after completing her bachelor's degree, she returned to school to earn her master's degree, then her PhD, in the medical field, all while working full time and raising two children. To her patients she is not only a health care provider but also a wealth of medical information and assistance, a facilitator of social services, a trusted advisor, a family mediator, and an all-around personal advocate. Lisa is an incredibly hardworking and determined person. She is many things to so many people. But she is not a good cook. Thankfully for everyone involved, her husband, Jim, is an artist in the kitchen.

Everything related to food has always been Jim's territory, from meal planning to grocery shopping to the actual cooking. His French toast recipe is rivaled only by his homemade apple sauce. Or beef tenderloin. Or made-from-scratch pies. Whenever I make a trip home to visit family, the luxury of family dinner made by Jim is one of my favorite things.

One evening when Jim was working late, Lisa realized she needed to feed their children *something* for dinner. Never being one to back down from a challenge, she surveyed the pantry, found some ingredients she knew how to assemble, and got back to work while the food was in the oven. As Lisa was pulling the dish from the oven, my niece Emma, who was about nine years old at the time, walked into the kitchen and asked, "Where is Dad?"

"At work," Lisa replied.

"Then who is going to feed us?" Emma genuinely wondered aloud, even as she saw the dish in Lisa's hands.

"I am," Lisa replied.

While Emma laughed out loud at the prospect of her mom cooking dinner, her five-year-old sister, Lizzy, loudly proclaimed, "*Girls* don't cook, silly! *Boys* cook!"

Why am I bothering to tell this story? What does this have to do with the role of women in the workplace and women in society in general? Perhaps nothing. Perhaps everything. We can learn a lot from a five-year-old.

The status of women in the workplace

There may not be a better source of information regarding the status of women in the workplace than the work being done by global management consulting firm McKinsey & Company. Before we dive into that work, though, a little background will help explain why we should trust what McKinsey's work is telling us. McKinsey is a global management consulting firm that operates in 135 cities in 67 countries, with over thirty thousand employees worldwide.[1] While McKinsey does not say this, ask around and you will hear it is one of the most—if not *the* most—prestigious and largest consulting companies in the world. It has the luxury of hiring the best and the brightest people from the world's most prestigious business schools.

Each year McKinsey, in partnership with LeanIn.org, conducts a comprehensive study of the progress of women in corporate America. LeanIn.org is a nonprofit organization founded by Sheryl Sandberg, billionaire, philanthropist, former chief operating officer of Facebook (now known as Meta Platforms), and *New York Times* best-selling author of *Lean In: Women, Work, and the Will to Lead*.[2] After finding great success as a senior executive at Google and later Facebook, Sheryl Sandberg founded LeanIn.org for the purposes of helping women achieve their ambitions and helping companies build inclusive workplaces where women of all identities are supported and empowered.[3] Together, McKinsey and LeanIn.org make a powerful authority on the status of women in the workplace.

Their most recent study, completed in 2022, was the largest study of women in corporate America that has ever been conducted. McKinsey collected information from 333 companies that collectively employ more than twelve million people. Over forty thousand employees of these companies were surveyed, with McKinsey conducting follow-up interviews with a cross section of female employees of diverse identities,[4] all in an effort to give us a clear picture of what is going on with women in the workplace across a broad range of companies today.

The findings are not encouraging. To quote from an article summarizing the McKinsey study:

> Despite modest gains in representation over the last eight years, women—and especially women of color—are still dramatically underrepresented in corporate America. And this is especially

true in senior leadership: only one in four C-suite leaders is a woman, and only one in 20 is a woman of color.[5]

(For those who aren't familiar with the corporate lingo, the term "C-suite" is a shorthand way of saying the most senior executive team of a company: the chief executive officer, chief operating officer, chief financial officer, chief legal officer, etc.)

Today in 2023, across companies of varying sizes, types, and characteristics in different geographic locations, women are still "dramatically underrepresented" in the corporate workplace. This isn't a problem that is limited to only a handful of industries or business sectors. The workplaces included in the study are as wide-ranging as asset management, banking, consumer goods, energy and utilities, engineering, health care, insurance, IT, media, manufacturing, pharmaceuticals, professional services (accounting, consulting, etc.), restaurants, retail, and technology.[6]

McKinsey's research shows that the percentage of women in management and leadership positions decreases dramatically at the senior levels of these companies. This would be discouraging enough if we were focusing on only the top role in the company: The chief executive officer. The statistics cover not just the CEO position, though. They include the entire senior executive teams of a broad range of companies across America.

One in four. Remember that statistic.

As a side note, I again fully recognize the terms "men" and "women" and "male" and "female" are not inclusive of all people. I fully recognize that gender is not binary and that categorizing people into just two groups is inherently flawed. I use the terms because that is what the data is based upon and, in general, the trends demonstrated by the data fall along traditional gender normative lines. While these categories are not fully inclusive, the data tells an extremely compelling story about the state of the workplace today.

Beyond the C-suite

It is not just the most senior-level positions in which women are drastically underrepresented. There are stark differences in gender parity throughout the corporate hierarchy. As you might expect, though, the lower the level of the position, the more women you will find. The higher the level of the position, the fewer women you will find.

At the entry level, for example, there is near gender parity, with women comprising 48 percent of the employee ranks.[7] This makes sense considering roughly one-half of the overall population is female. Why wouldn't roughly one-half of the workforce also be female? But we aren't talking about the entire workforce here. We are only talking about the entry level, the lower-level positions across corporate America. This data tells us that companies are hiring men and women in roughly equal numbers at the entry levels.

The gender parity disappears pretty quickly once you move up from the entry-level jobs. At the manager level, just one promotion up from the entry-level category (as categorized by McKinsey), the percentage of women drops to 40 percent.[8]

One level up, at the senior manager or director level, the percentage of women decreases to 36 percent.[9] Think about that fact for a moment. Nearly two-thirds of all senior managers and directors are men. That means corporate America is losing—or failing to promote in equal numbers—a significant percentage of women in the workforce after just a few levels of promotion.

The percentage of women continues to decline as we continue to climb up the corporate ladder. At the vice president level, the percentage of women drops to 32 percent, and at the senior vice president level the percentage of women declines to just 28 percent.[10] Said differently, at public and privately held companies of various sizes and types across the country, nearly three out of every four senior vice president roles are filled by men.

Of course, some companies and some industries outperform

these averages in terms of the retention and promotion of women. But some are worse.

What the data tells us is that, with the exception of entry-level jobs, women are vastly underrepresented in corporate America at all levels. And the percentage of women decreases at each level of promotion, beginning with the entry level up through the C-suite executive level.

Trends for the future

The current state of gender disparity in corporate America is discouraging. McKinsey's research found we have cause to be concerned for the future, as well. To quote again from the article summarizing these findings:

> Women leaders are leaving their companies at the highest rate we've ever seen—and at a much higher rate than men leaders. To put the scale of the problem in perspective: for every woman at the director level who gets promoted to the next level, two women directors are choosing to leave their company.[11]

The gender disparity problem is going to get worse. Possibly much worse. We know women are leaving their companies at record levels. Yes, some are leaving one company to join another. There will be winners and losers, so to speak, in the hiring and retention of women. Some companies and some industries will fare better than others. But it isn't just women changing employers; it is also women changing careers (meaning they will likely not have the same level of seniority after the change), and women leaving the corporate workplace altogether. Corporate America will either have to make meaningful changes to improve the retention and promotion of women or face the reality that women will continue to leave at high rates.

What is happening to all the women?

What is happening? Why are so many women leaving? And where are all of the women going?

These are complicated questions with no easy, neat answers. Women leave their jobs for varied and countless reasons, some of which are easy to identify and others that are not. Some reasons are unique to a person or situation and others are more common; some are cited by the women who leave and others go unsaid. Sometimes women (like me) don't have one or even a handful of reasons that led to their departure; it is more of a feeling of "I just need to quit." I've been there. Maybe you have, too. It can be difficult to pinpoint specific reasons. It is more of a culmination of circumstances, occurrences, and feelings that add up over time. There are no easy answers.

McKinsey distilled a few common themes to at least partially explain the trend of women leaving their companies in increasing numbers. First, McKinsey found that women leaders face stronger "headwinds" to advancement than men.[12] Women report experiencing microaggressions that undermine their authority, and many believe their gender or the fact that they have children played a role in being passed over for pay raises and promotions.[13] Second, McKinsey found that women leaders are "overworked and underrecognized."[14] While women leaders do more than their male peers to support employee well-being and foster diversity, equity, and inclusion, that work "is not formally rewarded in most companies" despite the fact that it "dramatically improves employee retention and satisfaction."[15] In other words, there is a silent burden of additional work being done by women that isn't rewarded. Third, McKinsey concluded that women leaders are seeking a "different culture of work," one that offers more flexibility or is more committed to employee well-being and diversity, equity, and inclusion.[16]

McKinsey found these factors to be even more important to

the next generation. Younger women (those under the age of thirty) are even more likely than current women leaders to prioritize flexible work arrangements and a company's commitment to employee well-being and diversity, equity, and inclusion.[17] The McKinsey study concluded that companies will struggle even more to recruit and retain the next generation of women leaders unless they take action to effectively change the course.[18]

My thoughts on why women leave

With so many brilliant minds already focused on the issue of the barriers to the advancement of women in the workplace, my purpose here is not to espouse some profound and different theory of why women are leaving or what can be done to retain and support them in their careers. Even I, one of the women who fled, can't fully explain it. But I can tell you what I saw for myself as a woman in the working world. I left my first company after seven years, before I was eligible for the big promotion I had been eyeing since the day I joined. Most of my female colleagues left the company long before I did. Some jumped ship as early as the one-year mark. Others stayed a couple of years, then left in search of a workplace that would provide more flexibility, shorter hours, and more emphasis on employee well-being. While most of the women I knew made the move to another company in the same or a similar industry, some left for completely different careers (thus losing the seniority they had built up). And some left the workforce entirely.

This pattern was not unique to the first company at which I worked. In keeping with the findings of the McKinsey study, I've watched this pattern play out throughout my career, both at companies at which I have worked and through my friends' experiences at other companies.

Knowing my own experiences and those of my friends and colleagues, I still can't explain why so many women leave or what can be done to improve the retention and promotion of women in any meaningful way. The reasons are too numerous, too complex, and too personal for me to draw conclusions, make generalizations, or attempt to speak for more than just myself. I can tell you that, for my friends, my female colleagues, and me, it had something to do with who we saw when we looked at the composition of the senior leadership. More accurately, it had a lot to do with who we did NOT see in senior leadership roles.

You can't be what you can't see

We can learn a lot from a five-year-old. To my then-five-year-old niece, it was normal for her father to cook all of the family meals. It was silly that her mother would attempt to make dinner. In my five-year-old niece's worldview, boys do the cooking.

Now imagine as this child grows up and joins the workforce (assuming, of course, she joins the traditional workforce of corporate America). Regardless of the company's size, revenue, number of employees, industry, or geographic location, we know some statistics about her future employer.

As she walks the halls of her company, she will notice (consciously or subconsciously) a great gender disparity in who occupies the mid- and senior-level positions. She will notice the disparity beginning just above her entry-level job, where at the manager level men occupy 60 percent of the positions. As she looks to the senior manager level, she will see that 64 percent of those positions are occupied by men. As she looks to the vice president level, she will notice the percentage of men rises to 68 percent.

As she dreams of a senior vice president role, she will notice the disparity gets even larger. She will see that 72 percent of the senior vice president positions are occupied by men. And as she dreams even bigger—because I know Lizzy and I know she will dream *that big*— she will see that men occupy three out of every four C-suite positions. Think about that for a moment. For every woman who makes it to the C-suite—whether it be the CEO, chief operating officer, chief financial officer, or some other C-level position—there will be three men who do the same.

Would it be silly for a young woman to think she could rise to the level of the C-suite? Or senior vice president? Or even vice president?

Imagine being that girl beginning her career with the knowledge of the statistical uphill battle that is the reality for women today. Would you believe you will be the exception to the rule? Would you believe you will be one of the few who defy the odds?

You can't be what you can't see.

Girls Who Code and other organizations have been working tirelessly to close the gender gap in technology and engineering. They are making progress. Their job is not done—far from it. But the problem is at least now widely recognized, and they have caught the attention of some of the largest technology companies in the world. We need to do the same in every profession where such a disparity still exists— and we know the gender disparity still exists pretty much everywhere when we look at senior-level positions.

The technology sector has Sheryl Sandberg and other heroic Gen-X women. Those of us in other professions need to find and identify our heroines. We need to champion their accomplishments. We need to recognize and honor the trailblazers who came before us and those who walk among us. We need to show the next generation of women that it *is* possible for them to reach the senior ranks of their chosen professions.

We need to inspire and equip the next generation of women to help them become what they might not yet be able to see. It isn't the whole solution, not by a long shot. But it's a start.

We need real change—from the top

We need corporate America to listen and truly understand what we are saying. We need them to understand what the data are saying. We need the people in senior leadership positions to make this a priority across all industries and companies. We need companies to make meaningful, actual change.

LeanIn.org and McKinsey have dedicated significant thought leadership, brainpower, and resources to this important issue. They are producing concrete suggestions, plans, and programs for how companies large and small, across all industries, can begin to effectuate meaningful improvements in the retention and promotion of women and other diverse people. We now need all companies to make the commitment to change the way business has always been done. We need them to level the playing field. For if they do not, they will continue to lose significant numbers of one-half of their employees (i.e., the women) before they reach the mid and senior leadership levels.

No business can be successful in the long term when it is losing significant numbers of its employees—and their unique talents and perspectives—every year. But this is the reality today. It becomes a constant cycle of having to recruit and hire new people to replace the ones who have left. Many companies clearly understand this and are dedicating resources and effectuating real change. Others are saying the right things, but the numbers are not moving, or at least not moving enough. When it comes to meaningful action that results in real change, some companies are falling silent.

What can we do about it?

We can keep preaching our message. We can keep making noise until those in leadership positions implement actions to improve the retention and promotion of women. We can demand that our own employers take this issue seriously. We can continue to bring these disparities to light whenever we see them.

We can keep sharing the statistics. We can keep spreading the message that gender disparity in corporate America is real and probably worse than most of us realized. We can point to the work of McKinsey and LeanIn.org as resources for leaders and companies that are committed to implementing change.

I want the next generation of women to look up and see a world that looks like them. I want them to see people in leadership positions who are male, female, and LGBTQIA+. I want them to see companies, industries, and an entire workforce that reflects who we are as a country. I want them to see senior leadership ranks comprising people of all genders, sexual orientations, races, ethnicities, national origins, religions, and disabilities. Only then will the youngest among them be able to look up and see themselves. Representation *matters*. You can't be what you can't see. My five-year-old niece taught me that.

In case you are wondering what happened to that ill-fated dinner, they threw it away and ordered a pizza instead. It turns out that, in this situation, the five-year-old was right all along. Some girls don't cook.

KEY TAKEAWAYS

- Women are vastly underrepresented in corporate America across all industries, business sectors, company sizes, business types, and geographic locations.

- Women in leadership roles are leaving their jobs at higher rates than they were in prior years, and at much higher rates than men.

- We need to keep spreading the word about the current state of gender disparity in the workplace. Demand that our own employers take this issue seriously and implement measures to effectuate real change.

- Until we have more equal gender representation across all levels of employees, it will continue to be difficult for young women to progress in their careers.

- You can't be what you can't see.

6

Don't Let Their Judgments Define You

People are going to judge you anyway, so
you might as well do what you want.

—TAYLOR SWIFT

It's a frequent, awkward conversation that starts with a time-filler question, like some bland elevator conversation about the weather.

"Do you have kids?"

The assumption is that I'll reply with "Yes, of course," after which I'll talk in some detail about the adorable little geniuses who inhabit my home. This cocktail party conversation happens a million times a day around the country, with no one really caring about the answer. That is, until the question is asked of someone like me.

"Do you have kids?"

"No."

"Really? Why not?"

"Why don't you have kids?"

I can't even begin to count how many times I've been asked this question. I am a middle-aged, married woman who does not have children. To many people, that makes me the object of curiosity. Or pity. Or maybe it makes me just plain weird.

I've had a successful career, first as a corporate lawyer and then as a professor. I serve on nonprofit boards and I raise money for causes about which I am passionate. I coached a national championship–winning cheerleading team. I run marathons. I've won awards. I wrote this awesome book. I have a great husband and incredible friends. But people rarely, if ever, ask me about any of these things in casual conversation.

Instead, I am asked the "why don't you have kids" question *all the time*. I am asked by acquaintances, coworkers, people I meet at cocktail parties, people I barely know, wives of my husband's colleagues, ladies at the nail salon, and strangers who sit next to me on airplanes. Even the checkout clerk at the grocery store once said, "You're making tacos for your kids tonight?" Nope. No kids. She looked straight at me and asked, "You don't have kids? Why don't you have kids?" I wish I was exaggerating. I wish I was making this up. But it is all completely true. I have been asked the dreaded question by all types of people in all types of places.

Judgment and pity

A few years ago, my husband and I were invited to a dinner event with some of his business colleagues and their spouses. I was seated next to one of his colleague's wives, someone I had met a few times over the years but did not know well. I knew her name, what neighborhood they lived in, and that she had two children. I didn't know much else about her or her family. I wouldn't call this person a friend or even an acquaintance, really. She was just someone I would see at parties or events from time to time. She was someone I might say hello to if I saw her at the grocery store, or maybe I would just walk by without recognizing her. After she talked nonstop about her children for at least fifteen minutes, she paused for a few seconds, then apologized and said, "Oh, I'm sorry, I forgot you don't have kids."

Then it got weird. I could practically hear the judgment inside of her head and braced myself for when it came spilling out of her mouth. Which it did. She literally said the following to me: "I feel so sorry for you. Your life must be so . . . empty . . . without children."

I could feel the fire raging inside of me. I wanted to get up and leave. I wanted to scream. How dare she judge my life as empty or sad? She doesn't even know me. She has no idea what my life is like. My life is pretty great, actually. And it is far from empty. I've worked at prestigious companies, collected promotions, built a great life with a great guy and some very spoiled pets, cultivated friendships with incredible women, volunteered for nonprofit organizations that serve the community, and immersed myself in the lives of my nieces and nephews. Yet this person, this woman who does not even know my last name (she incorrectly assumes it's the same as my husband's), who does not know me at all, felt it appropriate to judge my life as sad, lonely, and empty. To her, my life is worthy of nothing more than pity simply because I am not, like her, a mother.

What kind of society have we created if we view women not as successful but as pitiful, simply because they don't have children?

Judging only the women

Here is the really interesting thing: I don't think my husband has ever been asked the "Why don't you have kids" question. Not once. Why is that?

Why, as a society, are we so fixated on women having children? And why don't we have this same fixation when it comes to men? Why do people wonder "What's wrong with her?" if a woman doesn't have children but no one ever says that about men? No one seemed to care that George Clooney remained unmarried and without kids into his fifties. Contrast that with the media's obsession with women of the same generation who are unmarried or childless. Take Jennifer Aniston, for example. How many articles and blogs have talked about, speculated about, and wondered loudly about whether she will ever have kids, or why she doesn't yet have kids? How many have criticized her? How many have cast her as selfish or have said she chose her career over children? Google it. You'll find enough stories to fill at least four pages of search results. That in itself is incredibly telling.

Why is a woman's life viewed as incomplete if she is not married with children, while a man's life can be perfectly fulfilled by his career alone? Why don't we treat women and men equally when it comes to our collective views of marriage and children? Not everyone—and not every man—aspires to be a doctor, pastor, or internet mogul. So why do we assume every woman aspires to be a mother?

For everything my mom did to create a sense of strength and equality within me, she could not change the outside world. She could not shape societal views. She could not take away the judgment and inequality that I—and so many other women of my generation—would come to experience as adults.

Damned if you do, damned if you don't

In many ways our society has made great strides toward equality since the 1970s. Yet in many ways not much has changed. Every day, women are valued based on our relationships to men. We are measured by our marital status. We are judged by our maternal state. This is true whether or not a woman has a child. Judgment is not reserved only for the "sad" and "pitiful" people like me who chose not to have children. A fierce but entirely different type of judgment is cast upon those who are mothers.

Every day, women hesitate to announce pregnancies for fear it will negatively impact our careers. We fear being sidelined to the "mommy track." Women are viewed as somehow less dedicated to our careers, less available, or even less capable of competing in the professional world once we have children. Women struggle to preserve our careers during maternity leave and struggle even more after we return to the working world. We endure the snide comments of coworkers who joke about the "three-month vacation" (i.e., maternity leave) we take after the birth of a child. We constantly must prove that we are just as capable, just as dedicated, and just as motivated despite having a child.

Think about that for a minute. Some people in our society actually assume a woman somehow instantaneously becomes less capable at her job when she has a child. If you listen carefully, you may even hear someone say something along the lines of a woman being really good at her job "despite" having kids. Despite. There's that word again. It is as if some segment of our society would draw a Venn diagram with "professional success" in one circle, "mother" in another circle, and little overlap between them. Those same people are the ones who express surprise when they find a woman for whom those circles have intersected. Every day, many women are treated as if we are lesser in the professional world. It only gets worse once a woman becomes a mom. While some may not experience it on a daily basis or even at all, for others it is all too familiar. The bias is real. The judgment is real. The inequality is real.

Judgment is not reserved for working women with children, of course. Single women, divorced women, and married women without children are the subject of judgment, too, just of a different kind. Women are viewed as somehow lacking, less worthy, or someone to be pitied if we are not married with children. If you doubt this, look no further than the magazine rack at the grocery store. You will find no shortage of stories detailing which starlet is finally wearing a ring on *that* finger, or whose husband is cheating on her, or whether that forty-something actress will finally have a baby. It is as if society is saying a woman is not complete in her own right, that only marriage and children can complete her.

Women like Renee Zellweger and Sarah Paulson can win Oscar and Emmy awards. We can donate millions of dollars to vaccine research during a global pandemic, as Dolly Parton did. We can be international best-selling authors like Candace Bushnell. We can dedicate our lives and millions of dollars to building schools for girls who otherwise would not have access to education, as Oprah has done. We can become the vice president of the United States like Kamala Harris. All of these achievements will live beside the speculation, questions, and even the judgment by some segment of society of why that woman chose to live her accomplished life without having a child. All of her other achievements—regardless of how groundbreaking, trailblazing, and incredible they are—may never be enough for society until she is married with kids. Women continue to be judged by many according to an outdated ideal of what a woman's life is supposed to look like.

Stop defining women as wives and mothers

Let's stop defining women by their marital and parental status. Let's stop asking single women when they are finally going to find the "right guy." Let's stop feeling sorry for those who are divorced. Let's stop asking people like me why we don't have kids. Let's stop pressuring newlyweds with the "when are you going to have a baby" question. Let's stop treating maternity leave as a vacation and start seeing it for what it really is: exhaustingly difficult work. Let's stop assuming that working moms are less dedicated to their careers.

Let's all stop judging one another based on our marital and parental status. Let's stop viewing women as wives and mothers first, and professionals second. Instead let's just view women as equal people. Plain and simple. Because until we do all of that—until we stop measuring women based on marital and maternal status—women will never have an equal place in the world.

Why do we assume "happily ever after" must include a spouse and children? Why do we assume that single or divorced women must feel unfulfilled, regardless of their accomplishments? Why do we assume that mothers cannot be equally successful in the professional world?

As brilliantly summarized by Jennifer Aniston in an article that appeared in the *Huffington Post*, "We don't need to be married or mothers to be complete. We get to determine our own 'happily ever after' for ourselves."[1] When are we going to start believing that? When are we all going to start living that truth?

Create your own happily ever after

To the women of the world, it is time to create your own happily ever after. It is time for us to each define what completes our own lives. If you want to get married and have children, please do so. If you want to continue progressing in your career after having children, then make it happen. If you want to take a step back from your career to spend more time with your kids, more power to you. If you love your single life, stay single. If you are in a committed relationship but do not value the institution of marriage, stay just the way you are. If you are married but do not feel the desire to have children, please don't. For being a parent looks, to me, like the most difficult job in the world.

Be single. Be unmarried and in a committed relationship. Be married without children. Be married with children. Be something else altogether. I don't care which option you choose so long as you choose the option you really *want*. And live your choice proudly and without apology.

Please do not let others' perceptions or judgments define you or influence you. Do not bow to societal pressures or conventions. Define your own success. Create the life you truly want to live. If you have children, do not allow others to treat you as less capable in the workplace because of it. Stand up for yourself and for all women. Call out your coworkers and bosses when they insinuate you are not as dedicated to your job because you are also a mother. For the rest of us who do not have children, do not allow others to pity you. You have the right to be treated as equal regardless of whether you are single, divorced, married without children, married with children, or otherwise. Demand to be treated that way. Do not judge others based on the choices they have made or their life circumstances, which may not be a choice at all. Life is difficult enough without all that judgment.

Stop waiting for the perfect fairy-tale ending to play out. Buy your own glass slippers. Save yourself. And create your own happily ever after.

KEY TAKEAWAYS

- Women are constantly judged by an outdated ideal of what a woman's life is supposed to look like: that she should be married with children.

- Whether we have kids or not, all of us are being judged. Professional women with children are viewed by some as less committed to their careers or less capable of doing their jobs.

Professional women without children are viewed by some as selfish or too career-focused, or as having lives that are not complete. Men, in general, don't experience these same judgments.

- Do not let others' judgments or perceptions of what your life should look like influence or define you.

- We get to determine our own happily ever after.

7

Confronting
Locker Room Talk

Do we settle for the world as it is, or do we
work for the world as it should be?

—MICHELLE OBAMA

L ike most women I know (and plenty more whom I don't
know), I have experienced my share of sexism, bias, exclu-
sion, and inequality in the workplace. I got used to people
assuming I was someone's assistant just because I am female. I have
been called "sweetheart," "girl," "little lady," and a variety of other
demeaning terms by clients, coworkers, and men I interacted with
in business deals. I learned to ignore the occasional lewd joke or
crass comment. And I survived other, more serious instances of bias
and harassment.

But my experiences pale in comparison to the sexism, bias, and
outright discrimination endured by women of prior generations.
From the fight for women's suffrage in the early 1900s, to the battle

for equal rights under the law throughout the twentieth century, to the *Mad Men* era of blatant discrimination, the women who came before us forged a path on which we must now continue. To that end, I have spent the better part of the last few years writing about my experiences and sharing my insights and advice with the hope that these stories provide some guidance, support, and inspiration for the women of my generation and the generations that follow (that means you, Millennials and Gen-Z).

History teaches us that, with each generation that passes, the playing field becomes more and more level for women. With each generation the possibility for true gender equality becomes more attainable. That is, perhaps, until now . . .

A century of progress . . . then this . . .

The year was 2016. It is hard now to remember what life was like before we endured years of escalating events that polarized and divided the nation. It is hard now to recall an era when politicians acted in our best interest rather than simply voting against every single thing proposed by the other party. The year 2016 was the turning point, at least for me.

By the time the calendar turned from summer to fall, it seemed no one in this country was an undecided voter. Battle lines were drawn. The assault of political campaigns bombarded us constantly. Then, in an instant, we all became witnesses to an astounding thing. One month before the November election, a video leaked. Soon-to-become President Donald Trump was caught on camera boasting about sexually harassing and assaulting women.[1] We all saw (or heard, or read about) the presidential candidate bragging about his behavior. Laughing about it. Saying he could do "anything" he wanted to women. He used words I won't even put in print because I find them so offensive. I, like many other people, was stunned when I first saw the video. I was also sad, disappointed, and outraged that someone—and not just anyone, but a man running for president of the United States—could be so flippant and even proud of saying he can do "anything he wants" to women.

This, to me, was not just one video, but a commentary on how some men view women as possessions to be had, as challenges to be conquered, and as beings who have no choice but to submit to the desires of a man. This was just one example, just one symptom, of a much larger and more pervasive problem. It brought to our televisions and computer screens a live-action depiction of what so many of us have felt in our own lives but couldn't exactly describe: that at least some segment of society holds misogynistic beliefs that view women as less than equal, as a lower class, or as beings who don't deserve equal treatment.

Just as disturbing as the video itself was the public's reaction to it. While many people were disgusted and appalled by this behavior and attitude, many others ignored, overlooked, or discounted the video. "What's the big deal? It's just a video," was one common response I heard. "He's just bragging," was another common refrain. "It is just guys being guys, it doesn't mean anything." I heard that excuse a lot. Maybe these people honestly thought it wasn't a big deal. Maybe they believed he was just joking. But there is truth even in a joke. Maybe they were so drawn in by the promise of policy changes that they were willing to overlook the bad character on display.

The video was not an isolated incident, though. It was a pattern of behavior. For many months we witnessed the candidate making sexist comments to and about women ranging from news anchors to other presidential candidates (both Republican and Democrat) to talk show hosts and beauty queens. But the video . . . that was something entirely different.

Before you dismiss this as partisan rhetoric, I assure you I am not a diehard liberal. I am not even a Democrat. I've voted for Democrats, Republicans, and Independents. This is not about politics. Since the day that video leaked, I vowed to no longer sit by quietly and say nothing.

The real issue: normalized gender bias

This is about the movement that has grown within a segment of our country that reveals the hidden (or not-so-hidden) biases that exist. In the days and months following the release of the infamous video, the collective reaction was inconsistent. While many, including several prominent leaders in the Republican Party, condemned the video, many others did not. While influencers ranging from media personalities to professional athletes to movie stars loudly disavowed the offensive comments, others described it as just harmless talk.

Many people dismissed it as just "boys being boys." *That* is what this is about. It is about the hidden bias that has existed within society all along, only to reveal itself in the wake of the video's release. It is about recognizing and admitting that gender bias still exists today. It feels to me like that bias is stronger than I ever remember. It is about the bias being normalized, particularly when a person of great power and influence so blatantly flaunts it. That normalization empowered so many others to come out of the dark and say what they had previously kept in silence. There is power in numbers, after all.

We cannot dismiss the video or any similar comments, discussions, or talk as "locker room talk," as we were urged to do. "Locker room talk" is anything but just talk. It is not harmless. It is thought. It impacts those who hear it. It sends the message that men can do whatever they want to women. It is action. It is an indication of one's beliefs and thoughts. It exemplifies one's values. It is the demonstration of character. And it affects us all.

Turning back the clock on equality

Former First Lady Michelle Obama said it best in a speech she delivered in the days following the release of the infamous video:

> It reminds us of stories we heard from our mothers and grandmothers about how, back in their day, the boss could say and do whatever he pleased to the women in the office, and even though they worked so hard, jumped over every hurdle to prove themselves, it was never enough. We thought all of that was ancient history, didn't we? And so many have worked for so many years to end this kind of violence and abuse and disrespect, but here we are in 2016 and we're hearing these exact same things every day . . .[2]

I do not want to go back to the world of our mothers and grandmothers. I do not want to go back to a time in which the boss can say and do whatever he pleases to women. I do not want to return to an era in which I am not judged by my intellect or accomplishments, but by my gender. We, and the generations of women who came before us, have fought so hard to get to where we are today. Yet it feels like the clock is being turned back on us. On equality.

In 1920, the Nineteenth Amendment to the United States Constitution was ratified, thereby granting women the right to vote. Yet here we are, over one hundred years later, still fighting to be viewed as equal. To be treated as equal. To BE equal. Women will never be equal in the professional world, the community, or in our personal lives if we live in a society in which at least some segment so clearly views us as inferior.

If we accept the "locker room talk" explanation (whether with regard to the infamous video or any other instance in which any man makes a similar comment), then what message are we sending to women? To little girls and boys? To society as a whole? What can I possibly do or say that could help the next generation of women if we live in a world that views us as less than equal? What advice could I share, what encouragement could I give, if I know that young women are entering a professional world in which they can never fairly compete?

If you doubt that "locker room talk" is a symptom of a larger problem, then I ask you to check your social media feeds. Search Twitter, now known as X, for #repealthe19th. The "19th" refers to the Nineteenth Amendment. You will find a very long list of search results. Some days, the hashtag is trending. Quite literally the day I wrote this paragraph, people (and not just a few people) were using #repealthe19th in their posts in opposition of the confirmation of Judge Ketanji Brown Jackson to the United States Supreme Court. It isn't just this confirmation, or this judge, or this day, or even this year.

The hashtag has been trending, on and off, since 2016. You read that correctly. Enough people have been using the hashtag to make it trend at various times for at least the last seven years. At least some segment of society has been openly and publicly promoting the idea of taking the right to vote away from women. If this alone does not signify that "locker room talk" is more than just talk, I don't know what else I can say.

This is about equality

This is not about politics. This is not about a particular politician, a particular election, or a particular period of time. This problem has not gone away just because the election cycle moved on. Much the opposite, in fact. This is about gender equality and how bias is being normalized. It is about stopping the microaggressions. It is about calling out bias and sexist thoughts, beliefs, and actions wherever and whenever we see them.

This is not about Republicans versus Democrats, nor about ideology. This is not a matter of national security, foreign policy, or the economy. Yet it just might be the most important issue on which we must decide future elections.

This is about equality. Respect. Humanity. Moral character. It is about the centuries-long fight for gender equality and our obligation to past and future generations to ensure we do not go backward in time. This is about continuing the fight for ALL people to be treated with equal respect and dignity. This is about rooting out all types of discrimination. The fight for equality is far from over.

This is about recognizing and admitting that gender bias still exists and about combatting that bias. This is about having the courage to stand up for what is decent, what is moral, and what is right. To the women, men, and all people of the next generations, I promise you this: I will keep using my voice. I hope you do, too.

KEY TAKEAWAYS

- Talk is not harmless. If we allow excuses to permeate, we are giving a voice to and legitimizing the underlying gender bias.

- We will never achieve gender parity or equality in the workplace until women are treated as equal people in society.

- Despite all the gains in the fight for gender equality over the last one hundred years, the battle is not over. It is now our turn to fight for ourselves, each other, and the future.

8

Speak Your Truth

Whenever it feels uncomfortable to tell the truth,
that's often the most important time to tell it.

—JENNIFER LOPEZ

L ocker room talk. I wish I could say it is something I've only seen and heard about as the events of 2016 and the aftermath unfolded. But that would not be the truth.

Sometimes the truth is a very uncomfortable thing. Sometimes it is denied by others. Sometimes telling the truth means we provoke the aggressors, we piss off some people, and we might even make some enemies. So sometimes we bury, ignore, silence, or even try to forget the truth. But at some point, we feel compelled to speak out. We speak out not only for ourselves, but also for all the women and girls who come after us.

What follows are true tales taken from my own life. I've chosen not to name the people involved because this is not about specific people (no matter how bad their actions may have been). This is about a pervasive problem that exists in far too many workplaces even today. The actors in my (true) stories are merely proxies for the scores of men who commit similar acts every day across corporate America. For the most part, I've also chosen to disguise the companies and the time periods in which these events took place. If I named names, it would turn the focus to those specific people and places. And this problem is so much larger than that.

What I have experienced is not unique. My female friends, and an untold number of other women in corporate America, have similar—or even more harrowing—stories they could tell. It is for them, for you, and for myself that I share what follows. This is my truth.

The little things

When I started my first job, it wasn't a surprise that the majority of my coworkers were men. I knew that women held less than 20 percent of the senior-level positions. I knew the executive management team consisted entirely of white men. I knew that in an office of roughly 250 professionals, there were very few people of color. And as far as I knew, there were zero openly LGBTQIA+ people (but to be fair, it was a different time; same-sex marriage wouldn't even be legalized for more than a decade). I knew I was entering a very white, male-centric, traditional culture. None of this was unique to my company, though. It was, and to a great extent still is, an industry-wide problem in my chosen field and others. What I failed to understand, though, was how much the culture of a male-dominated industry would impact my daily life for the remainder of my career.

Signs of things to come

The first sign of things to come came in the form of a nice person who knocked on my office door during my first week of my first job.

Let's call her Stephanie. Stephanie introduced herself and welcomed me. Many of the people whose offices surrounded mine didn't have time to even stop to say hello as they zoomed down the hallway. I liked Stephanie immediately. Her reputation preceded her. I had already heard about her whip-smart intellect, her huge potential, and of course the fact that she was somehow holding down a successful career while raising two kids. Stephanie's office was on the opposite end of the floor from mine, separated by other offices, cubicles, conference rooms, and a bank of elevators. In other words, we wouldn't have casually run into each other very often. It was clear she had gone out of her way to find me, and I was flattered. After some chitchat about how I was finding things so far, Stephanie lobbed what should have been a red flag. She said, "I heard we hired another woman on this floor. I had to come meet you. I've been the only one here for a while." Did I think it was odd that, on a floor of roughly forty offices in a downtown high-rise, only one other office was occupied by a woman? Yes, I did. Did I think it was a little concerning that she'd been the only one there for a while? Yes, I did. But I didn't realize this was a harbinger of what I would experience in the future—and not just at that company.

Comments and non-invitations

Any single thing in isolation might seem like no big deal. Any single comment, or look, or instance of unequal treatment, or crude joke, or weird interaction could be dismissed. But, as I suspect nearly every woman knows, it is never just one comment. Or look. Or instance of inequality. It is the cumulative weight of these seemingly small things that eventually breaks the camel's back.

As just one example of a small thing, consider this. At one stop along my career path, my male coworkers went out to lunch together every Friday. Starting around 11:45 a.m., one guy would walk the floor to gather up all the others. They'd walk straight past my office, joking and laughing, without even turning their heads to glance in at me. It was like I was invisible. Every guy on the floor would get the lunch invite. But not me or any other women (and there were only a few of us). When summer rolled around, the same phenomenon took place with the invitations to play golf. The senior-level guys would invite the junior-level guys to join them for afternoons at their country clubs. Afternoons sometimes turned into evenings, with the guys staying for dinner, drinks, and relationship-building. But I never got the invite. Not even once. This happened frequently throughout my career, and not just at one company. My girlfriends who worked at other companies and in other industries experienced very much the same thing.

Some might view these as trivial examples, nothing more than coworkers socializing together. Some might say I was/am overly sensitive. Some might think it's no big deal. And to be honest, I really didn't want to do those things anyway. But the message was clear. I didn't belong and I would never be truly accepted as one of them.

While they were busy becoming buddies on the golf course, I was back at the office getting shit done. I thought I was the one who would come out ahead in this game. I was working while they were playing. I was learning, spending time with clients, improving my skills, and getting ahead. Or so I thought. What I didn't realize was the impact those relationships would have on *everything*. From who gets the career-building opportunities, to who gets handed down the client relationships, to who is chosen for the limited number of big promotions . . . relationships matter. They matter *a lot*. Spoiler alert: the winner in the game of work wasn't the girl who was back at the office while all the guys played.

Messages from leadership

Let me share a more obvious example. Once I was in the audience of maybe seventy-five employees at a mandatory training session for one company at which I worked. A senior leader said (and included in his PowerPoint) that women should never wear the color red. He explained that, if a woman wears red, it draws attention to the fact that she is a woman. Wear black or blue, he said. Don't wear jewelry, he said. Tone down the makeup, too. And don't act too feminine. The message was clear: To be successful, a woman must make everyone forget she is female. Being a woman is a negative, at least in that guy's opinion. We were told we needed to do what we could to make the men ignore or forget our gender difference.

Around the same time, I was scolded by a different senior-level guy for clearing coffee cups from a conference room table. He explained that I needed to be extra careful to avoid doing "female" things (presumably because it is a woman's job to do the dishes). He said he was sharing this advice because he wanted me to be successful. He thought he was one of the good guys. He thought he was helping me. The underlying message was loud and clear, though: women are not viewed as equal in the workplace; therefore, we need to avoid doing anything that reminds men of our gender. Even something as small as throwing away coffee cups would be too much of a reminder that I wasn't one of the guys.

The not-so-little things

The non-invites, the small comments, the gendered thinking leading to gendered actions—these types of seemingly small things happened. A lot. And every so often, it was something bigger.

Company events and strip clubs

Fast forward to another company training program in another city. This one took place over a weekend. Employees from the company's offices around the country had flown in for the event. I don't know how many people were in attendance, but the tables filled a hotel ballroom.

The sessions on Saturday were uneventful right up until the last few minutes. After the final presenter concluded, a senior-level guy stepped up to the podium and took the microphone. He ran through the logistics for the evening: cocktails at X bar at Y time, dinner at X restaurant at Y time . . . boring stuff. I was about to tune out the rest of the babble when his closing sentence jolted me back to attention. Even now, I remember what he said word for word: "And for after dinner, [male coworker whom I choose not to name here] is leading the charge. Be sure to bring your dollar bills so you can tip the entertainment."

By "entertainment," he meant the young women who worked at the local strip clubs. I know this for sure because the next morning I had the unfortunate luck of sitting at a breakfast table with some very hungover guys, including the one responsible for "leading the charge" the night prior. The guys couldn't stop laughing and talking about what went down at the strip clubs: Who passed out, how many dollar bills they stuck into the strippers' thongs (their words, not mine), who almost got kicked out, and how some of them hadn't slept yet. One guy joked he was going to submit the drink tab on his expense report but, unfortunately, couldn't include the dollar bills. I couldn't believe I had to spend my weekend with these overage frat boys bragging about their strip club antics. I didn't say anything at the time (which I now regret). I was relatively new to the company. I was the only woman at the table. All of the guys outranked me. They held all the power. I made the calculated decision to keep my mouth shut and just get the hell out of there as fast as I could.

I'm not sure what part of this unfortunately true story I find most offensive: that my coworkers went to a strip club during a work event weekend, that they thought it was perfectly fine to brag about it at the breakfast table, or that a senior leader thought it was appropriate to stand on a stage in a hotel ballroom full of employees and tell them to bring their dollar bills for the entertainment. I'll let you decide.

The elevator incident

About a month after I started working at one company, I was in the elevator with a female friend who worked on another floor. She and I met up for lunch or lattes as often as possible. I was wearing black bootcut pants, a black suit jacket, a white button-down shirt, and black stack-heeled booties. My shoulder-length bob was tucked behind my ears. The only jewelry I wore was my wedding ring. My friend was wearing a tweed riding jacket, a tea-length taupe-colored wool skirt, and knee-high brown leather boots. Her long hair was pulled back in a low ponytail and she wore small hoop earrings but no other jewelry. We were not dressed for the nightclubs. It was all business, and we were doing our best not to make our femaleness stand out. We played by the rules we thought we had to follow, no matter how biased and shitty those rules were.

Before you judge our fashion choices, I'd like to point out this was the dawn of the new millennium, the era of Britney Spears and her super-low-rise jeans, zigzag-parted hair, and every female celebrity from J. Lo to Paris Hilton dressed in Juicy Couture velour tracksuits. Yes, I was the very proud owner of much Juicy attire, along with a closet full of baby Ts and low-rise True Religion jeans. But this was work, so we had to tone it down. Way down. In came the pantsuits and equestrian-themed tweed.

As we rode the elevator up from the lobby cradling our lattes, the doors opened to let in another passenger: A very senior-level, older man. This person occupied a corner office. He was both revered and feared, and was known to have made the careers of more than a few of our colleagues. He didn't know us, of course. But we knew who he was. It was in one's best interest to know when one is in the presence of someone of this level.

He entered the elevator, smiled, then looked us up and down from the tips of our shoes to the tops of our heads. He wasn't discreet about it. His chin moved up and down as he scanned us from top to bottom. Just smile and be nice, I reminded myself. He's a very big deal at this company. That's when he said what he thought was an okay thing to say to two women who were half his age. "What is it with you girls wearing pants and long skirts?" he said. Stumbling for words, my friend said something about it being cold outside. He replied, "Well, what am I supposed to look at?" I was speechless. I couldn't come up with a reply, even if I would have had the guts to tell him how inappropriate his comment (and his scanning of our bodies) was. My friend and I both stood there in silence, awkwardly smiling, until the elevator doors opened and we escaped.

I wish I could say that was the only time I was made to feel incredibly uncomfortable by the words or actions of a very senior, very important older man. But it wasn't.

The bigger things

Shortly after I joined another company, I met another very senior-level, very powerful older man. He had a long history with the company, close relationships with some of the company's biggest clients, and a reputation for being the type of person who could make or break someone's career. He wielded his power openly, always wanting to be sure we all knew exactly how important he was. Let's call him the Very Important Person.

I quickly learned there was a pattern to the Very Important Person's work habits and behaviors. As the one leading the project teams for some of the most important clients, he had the authority to staff those teams with whichever junior, mid-level, and management-level people he chose. Let's just say the percentage of women on the projects he led far exceeded the percentage of women in the office overall. Women (usually the prettier ones) across various disciplines and areas of expertise were always selected. Fairly early on, I, too, became part of some of those teams.

At first, I chose to think of it as an opportunity for us women to get valuable experience and exposure to important clients. I chose to view it as a reflection of my work product, not a commentary on my looks. But over time, it became harder and harder to ignore what was really going on.

Beware of the Very Important Person

The other women and I traded some tips for how to deal with the Very Important Person (and other very important men at the company). We never got into a real discussion about his inappropriate words and actions, though. We didn't know each other that well and, at least for me, I wasn't entirely sure whom I could trust. I didn't want to be pegged as the one talking shit about the Very Important Person. We resorted to quick comments and "Hey, be careful" statements, but not much else.

There would have been strength in numbers. But we were from different areas of expertise in the company, and there wasn't a constant, cohesive group of women working together. The Very Important Person kept our interactions largely separate. He rotated which women were involved in which project teams. By keeping us siloed from one another, he kept us from building the kind of relationships that could have led to trust and collective action. We did as much as we felt comfortable doing to help one another. But we never felt comfortable enough to have deep, meaningful conversations about what we individually had experienced. And so, we did what we could to protect ourselves and each other without exposing ourselves to backlash. Of course, none of this should have been necessary. But it was.

Be aware he will call you into his office, tell you to sit down, then remain standing while he looks down at you the entire time. Don't be intimidated; he does this to everyone (or, at least, to all the women). Wear turtlenecks, crewnecks, or shirts with high necklines. He will stare at your boobs anyway, but at least you won't feel so exposed. Don't wear skirts or dresses so he can't stare at your legs. Never wear anything that's tight or very fitted. Carry your laptop or a notebook like you're hugging it in front of your chest, arms crossed around it. That way he can't stare directly at your boobs. When walking down the hall, slow your pace so he will walk next to or ahead of you. That way you won't have to feel him staring at your butt. Bring an extra copy of any document in case he "forgets" his. You don't want him leaning over you to share your laptop or your document. He's going to make some comments that are slightly inappropriate (but not blatantly so). It isn't your imagination and you aren't overreacting. He is careful in the words he chooses but his words are cringey enough that you'll feel uncomfortable. Don't engage, don't reply, and don't let him know it bothers you. Act like you didn't hear what he said. Maybe even say, "I didn't hear you. Can you please repeat that?" That should shut him up. Try to find an ally in another guy on the team. Let that guy know you'd rather not sit next to the Very Important Person (in meetings, on airplanes, or anywhere else). If he is one of the decent ones, he will always take the seat next to the Very Important Person.

While he will never know it, to this day I am grateful for a certain former college football player colleague of mine who always, always took the seat next to the Very Important Person without me even having to ask.

Maybe I (and the other women) didn't need to be this on guard around the Very Important Person. Maybe my self-imposed rules were overkill. But I wasn't interested in finding out. I did what I thought I had to do to make the environment tolerable so I could keep doing my job. I had a career to build, and I wasn't going to let one man and his lingering stares and awkward comments derail my plans.

The ombudsperson

At some point, though, I had had enough. It wasn't just the Very Important Person. There were instances—many instances—similar to the ones I mentioned earlier happening to me and also to my female colleagues at this particular company.

At some point I decided I needed to move to a different department within the company. Or I needed to quit. I don't even remember what it was that pushed me to that point. I don't think it was any single thing, just the culmination of too many little things. My endurance was depleted and I needed help.

Before I explain what happened next, I need to tell you a little more about me. Despite the fact that I'm now sharing my entire story with complete strangers, I am not an extrovert or outspoken person. I say "Excuse me" nicely to strangers on the street, even when they are the ones who bump into me. I apologize for things that aren't my fault. All the time. I don't ask for help from anyone . . . pretty much ever. I don't think I have ever sent my food back to the kitchen at a restaurant. I never complain to a store manager even when an employee is overtly and absurdly rude. Each time I've quit a job, I was internally terrified to tell my boss I was leaving. I hate confrontation. And I've spent most of my life trying to please my parents, teachers, coaches, and bosses.

But at some point, even I couldn't take it anymore.

The company had a designated ombudsperson, a senior-level leader that any employee could go to with concerns, issues, or complaints. The ombudsperson was not in the human resources group, nor was she in any reporting relationship to the department heads or senior management. She was a heavy hitter, a rare female who had risen to prominence against all odds of her Baby Boomer generation. In other words, her voice and her opinion mattered. A lot. People listened to her, and she could make things happen.

The ombudsperson role was a way for employees to confidentially report a problem without having to go through the normal chain of command and without having to worry about retaliation. This was a pretty revolutionary thing at the time. At many companies, there was no hotline, no ethics officer, no whistleblower number, and no corporate compliance path to report instances of harassment, discrimination, inappropriate behavior, ethics violation, or other problem. In this regard, I'm happy to say my company was cutting-edge.

After a very bad day (which I don't even remember, other than it was very bad), I knew it was time. I waited until later in the evening when my presence on the floor where the ombudsperson's office was would be less obvious. I pressed the elevator button with my shaking hand. I put one foot in front of the other, with my heart beating so loudly I could almost hear it, until I stood in front of the ombudsperson's office door. She was alone, not on the telephone, and didn't appear to be too busy. It's now or never, I thought. I reminded myself I had done nothing wrong; the wrongs had been done *to* me, not *by* me. I took a deep breath, knocked on the door, and asked if she had a few minutes to talk about something important (to me).

She invited me in. She was warm and welcoming. I could almost feel the relief coming over my body. I sat down, opened my mouth, and let the words pour out. It was completely out of character for me to have the guts to tell a senior leader, someone the age of my parents and someone who had worked at the company for her entire career, all the things I thought were wrong with the place. I told her about the crude comments. I told her how I was excluded and treated differently because of my gender. I told her as many of the "little things" as I could remember, but I didn't tell her about the Very Important Person. Not yet.

Much to my surprise, she understood. Completely. She told me what life was like for her when she started her career. She talked about how difficult it was to be a young female professional in the 1970s and 1980s. It sounded like something out of a *Mad Men* episode, and I was not envious. I understood things were much worse for her generation. But that didn't change the fact that I was sitting in the middle of a pretty bad situation myself. I needed something to be *done* about it.

She wasn't getting the seriousness of my story. So I told her I couldn't stay working in my current department. Again, to my surprise, she understood. But she said we needed more time. We needed a plan. I couldn't just move to another area of the company because that would leave my old team short-staffed. Serving the clients' needs came first. My fragile self would have to be patient. I said I'd try.

When nothing happened after a few weeks, I made the trip up to her office again. This time I didn't hold back. At all. I told her about my interactions with the Very Important Person. I told her how uncomfortable he made me (and others). I described the staring at my boobs, the comments on my legs, and how he'd sit too close and lean over too far. That's when the conversation went a direction I simply was not expecting. "Oh, that's just [Very Important Person's name]. He's harmless," she said.

Wait. What?

That was it. End of conversation.

I was going to have to make things happen for myself. So that's what I did. By that time, I had met several people from another department in the company, an area where I had zero experience. I knew nothing about the work they did but I liked the people. They were much more laid-back, friendlier, and less overtly competitive. They were more my kind of people. And they were *busy*. I mean, they were swamped with work and actively interviewing candidates to join them. I reached out to one of the people whom I'd met a few times. He wasn't in charge of that group, but he held a fairly senior-level position. We talked. Then talked some more. Then things started to happen. This person went to bat for me for the first time then, and many more times over the years. Once he got involved, shit got done.

I had a new role in the company within a few weeks. But before that happened, I was called into a meeting with the head of my old department. He questioned me about why I wanted to make the move. He lectured me about what a big mistake I was making for my career. He sternly said he couldn't allow me to move until he had time to hire additional staff, a process he said would take six to nine months. He said I would have to stay put out of fairness to the rest of the team. That's what he was concerned about—the rest of the team. He wasn't concerned about any of the unequal treatment or inappropriate behaviors I had experienced.

That's when I, a terrified and intimidated person sitting in the shadow of one of the most powerful men in the company, played the only cards I had left. I said I had been talking with the ombudsperson about my experiences. I said she could fill him in on the details. As for his suggestion that I'd have to wait six to nine months to make a move, I told him I would quit immediately if I had to stay in my current situation. He said he'd consider all of this and get back to me. Then he motioned toward his office door and told me I could leave.

To be honest, I have no idea where I got the guts to say any of that. It is very out of character for me to stand up to anyone of authority, let alone the guy in charge. But I had nothing to lose. It was that or quit, and I wasn't willing to quit without a fight. A few days later I got an email from him, copying the ombudsperson and the leader of my new team, saying my move would be effective the following week.

Life wasn't perfect after that, but it was a hell of a lot better. I still had to deal with the Very Important Person here and there. But not every month or even every year. Gone were the weird comments, the gawking, and the uncomfortable situations (at least for me). I like to think my reporting to the ombudsperson changed things for the women in that department. But I don't know that for sure. I did what I had to do to save myself. I utilized the tools I had, including reporting the harassment. It was now in their hands to fix the problem. I could move on with my career and my life knowing I had done what I could, and I had done what's right . . . not just for myself, but for other women.

The message

Over the years I endured my share of crude jokes, awkward comments, blatant stares at my boobs and legs, absent invitations, and other microaggressions that, over time, added up to *a lot*. I think a lot of women have. And every once in a while, I endured something more. Something worse. Something that, looking back, seems like it was taken from the 1950s and not the 2000s.

None of this—the inappropriate comments, the advice to disguise my gender, the rules on what to wear or how to act, the non-invitations, the strip clubs, the rules I had surrounding the Very Important Person—none of this should have happened. None of this behavior was acceptable, normal, or should have been tolerated by anyone. No single thing stands out as *that* big of a deal. We tolerate it. But should we have to? Of course not.

But this was my reality, and I dealt with it the best way I could. I kept my career on track. I took the opportunities to be on project teams for high-profile clients. I learned and absorbed as much as I could. I gained knowledge and skills. I had opportunities to level up my work experience that I wouldn't have otherwise had. And I kept my distance (as much as possible) from the bad behavior while doing it.

This, my friends, is exactly why I feel obligated to tell these stories. It isn't fun or at all comfortable to relive the experiences or feelings. I'm not making any friends by airing this for the public to read. At least some of what I've said is bound to piss some people off. Still, I feel obligated and compelled to speak these truths because I don't want any present or future generations of women to have to endure what I did just to keep their careers intact and on track.

I feel obligated and compelled to share these stories until there are no more women left who have similar stories to tell.

KEY TAKEAWAYS

- While corporate America has made significant progress, there is more work to do.

- Gen-X women (in their forties and fifties today) experienced our share of bias, inequity, discrimination, and harassment in the workplace. Even today, women of all ages still experience those things.

- Let's keep sharing our stories, speaking our truths, and continuing the discussions so the working world will be a better place for the women of today and tomorrow.

9

It Takes More Than Grit

Grit (grit) *noun.*

1.a) sand, gravel

  b) a hard sharp granule (as of sand)
    also: material (as many abrasives)
    composed of such granules

2.any of several sandstones

3.a) the structure of a stone that adapts to its grinding

  b) the size of abrasive particles usually
    expressed as their mesh

4.firmness of mind or spirit: unyielding courage
  in the face of hardship or danger // [he]
  managed to survive by his grit and guile

5.capitalized: a Liberal in Canadian politics

—MERRIAM-WEBSTER DICTIONARY[1]

G rit. It's a popular term. It is a term we've all heard. Maybe even too much. Business leaders love to talk about it. Academics study it; some even make careers out of it. Consultants espouse its importance. TED Talk speakers, authors, consultants, and thought leaders preach it, dissect it, explain it, and redefine it.

Grit is held up as the key trait that leads to success. It is the holy grail of attributes and the thing we all should aspire to have, learn, and practice. Talent, intelligence, and experience are important. But the world seems to be telling us that grit is the most important factor of all. Many argue it is the most accurate predictor of success in the working world, more than a person's education, experience, personality, professional network, or intelligence. This isn't limited to success in the professional world, of course. Grit is also talked about (a lot) in education, the arts, games, hobbies, and of course, sports. Simply put, if you are looking for *the* thing, the X factor, the "it" that makes some people more successful than others, that thing is grit. And, presumably, if someone isn't successful or isn't achieving what we would expect, then maybe grit (or more accurately, lack of grit) is the reason why. Then again, maybe not.

Defining grit

What is grit? What does it really mean to say someone has (or doesn't have) enough grit? The Merriam-Webster Dictionary defines grit as "firmness of mind or spirit; unyielding courage in the face of hardship or danger." Firmness of mind and unyielding courage sound like great things to me. I'd like to have those. We could all use a little more courage, especially when we are faced with really hard things. But what does that really *mean* in our day-to-day lives? And what does it have to do with us being successful (or not) in our academic pursuits and professional careers?

Perhaps the most recognized authority on the topic of grit is Angela Duckworth, PhD, professor, *New York Times* best-selling author, podcast host, nonprofit founder, consultant, and presenter of one of the most-viewed TED Talks of all time.[2] Dr. Duckworth defines grit as "passion and perseverance for long-term goals."[3] She describes it as a certain mindset toward "a goal you care about so much that it organizes and gives meaning to almost everything you do. And grit is holding steadfast to that goal. Even when you fall down. Even when you screw up. Even when progress toward that goal is halting or slow."[4]

After reading Dr. Duckworth's work and thinking about it (a lot), I think I understand the concept of grit. To me, grit means having the ability to stick with it, to focus on the end goal, and to push through obstacles. It is the capacity to see a problem as only a temporary road-block that can be overcome, rather than allowing that problem to stop your forward motion. It is believing one can push through a challenge and still achieve the end goal in spite of the problems that come up along the way. It is perseverance. Determination. Resilience. The ability to prioritize the thing you are passionate about above all else. In the words of the gymnastics coaches of my childhood, it is the ability to push through the pain. To dig deep. To never lose focus on the end goal.

To be fair, this is only an incredibly cursory summary of what grit means and the science behind it. Dr. Duckworth and others have written entire books on the topic, not to mention the podcasts, TED Talks, websites, academic articles, blogs, keynote speeches, workbooks, courses, and much more. If the topic of grit is of interest to you, you may want to start with Dr. Duckworth's work. There is a very good reason her books achieve instant *New York Times* best-seller status.

My purpose here is not to summarize—or even begin to explain—the volumes of material that have been published on the topic of grit. My purpose is much smaller: to think about grit as an important thing, but not THE thing. To counteract some of the thought around grit that is making women feel like they just don't have it, whatever "it" is. To give women, and in particular younger women in the earlier stages of their careers, some perspective on how to think about grit—especially if they are being told it's something they lack.

How much does grit matter?

My real question is this: How much does grit truly matter? When compared to the multitude of institutional, cultural, and systemic barriers that some people face, is grit really the most accurate predictor of success? And why are business leaders, academics, thought leaders, and consultants to the corporate world so focused on infusing the concept of grit into our lexicon and our collective thinking? Might the focus on grit be distracting us from other truths, some of which aren't particularly positive or appealing to uncover? In other words, if we are so focused on the concept of grit, are we ignoring external factors that are pushing some toward success and others toward failure?

The experts would tell you grit is a critical trait that successful people have in common. It is the thing that separates high achieving people from the rest of us. And they would tell you that you need not panic if you do not possess enough grit. Grit can be learned. Grit can be taught, developed, and increased. Some thought leaders equate it to a muscle that can be conditioned to grow stronger. If you can understand what it is, learn how to gain some amount of it, and work to strengthen it, you can become better, more resilient, and more successful.

If grit is the most important indicator of—and ingredient to—success, and if grit can be learned and strengthened over time, then that means our ability to succeed is largely within our own control. But is that really true? Should we be so focused on grit? And if we are, is the focus on grit keeping us from seeing some other truths?

What if grit isn't the determining factor?

I am a true believer that some people have it, whatever "it" is. I know it when I see it. Some people have the innate ability to endure more, tolerate more, work harder, work longer, grind more, focus more, push through, and get shit done in circumstances under which most people would give up. Some people are more determined. Some can endure things that would make others crumble. Some can just keep pushing. And pushing. And pushing. Does that mean these people have more grit than the rest of us? Should we all want more of that? And will having that make us successful?

People flourish under different circumstances. People crumble under different conditions. That is all true. We are inherently different beings with different strengths, weaknesses, personality traits, attributes, core beliefs, priorities, demands on our time, and a million other differences that I haven't mentioned. All of those, in varying degrees, impact how each of us handles the pressure, stress, obstacles, problems, personalities, and the daily grind of the professional world.

Yes, I believe that grit exists. Yes, I acknowledge that some people have "it," the X factor that makes a big difference. But in my humble opinion, that one factor does not explain or determine success. There are a million reasons why one person may succeed where another does not. There are countless circumstances that will either push us forward or slow us down. There are external factors we can't control, regardless of how much grit we have.

Here, then, is my real question: how much do factors that are beyond our control impact our potential for success, regardless of how high a person rates on the grit scale?

As compared to the impact of grit, how much do factors like socioeconomic background, educational opportunities, systemic barriers, discrimination, inequality, and other things beyond our control determine a person's potential for success? Don't these factors have at least as much of an impact as grit has on our ability to achieve?

The unequal playing field

From a very young age we are taught, conditioned, and raised to believe that life is basically fair. We all grew up playing games. Whether it was a neighborhood game of tag, or competitive sports, or board games, or academic competitions, or even the simple act of forming a line on the playground, we all grew up playing games of some kind, each with a distinct set of rules. We are taught that rules are to be followed. Break the rules and get penalized; follow the rules and move on to the next square. As children, we are taught in this way to think each person's destiny is within their control.

We are also taught to believe that everyone starts at the same line and everyone's finish line is the same distance away. We know that the person who crosses the finish line first, or scores the most points, or answers the most questions correctly, is the fair winner. After all, no one has a shorter racetrack in the 100-meter sprint.

It is logical, then, for us to think that is also true in the adult world. That we all have an equal shot in the race of life. But the brutal and honest truth is that life is not fair. We do not all have the same starting line and finish line. We are not all running the same race. Not even close.

As long as we think the race is fair, though, we will believe that failure to finish first is our own fault. We will continue to believe it is our shortcomings that caused the result. We will assume our lack of grit is the reason we didn't win. We will blame ourselves, doubt ourselves, and eventually lose faith in ourselves.

But what if we viewed things differently? What if, instead of assuming we lack the requisite amount of grit to achieve our end goals, we instead weigh the attribute of grit alongside all the other factors at play and examine the other possible barriers to success? What if grit is not the primary reason we succeed or fail? What if, instead, we view it as just one contributing factor in a much more complicated puzzle? What if there are other pieces that play a much bigger part?

One example: wealth

Yes, we can control some things. Others we simply cannot. No matter how much grit one does or does not possess, some things may be out of our reach. Consider for a moment two people: one born into great wealth and privilege, the other not. The grit factor alone—or even predominantly—can't predict or even largely determine the success of either person.

The one born into great wealth and privilege could lack any meaningful amount of grit yet still progress through elementary school, high school, college, and at least the early years of their career looking pretty successful. At the risk of making some massive generalizations and probably unfair assumptions about how people of great wealth and privilege live and raise their children, stay with me while I do exactly that.

Children who are raised in wealthy, privileged families likely have had the advantages of good schools and safe neighborhoods; access to resources, extracurricular activities, sports, the arts, and educational assistance (i.e., tutors and test prep courses); and connections to other wealthy and privileged family and friends who can make introductions and open doors for them. Of course, this is not true of every person who was born into wealth and privilege. But at a minimum, I think we can all agree that children from wealthy and privileged families tend to have much better access to basic needs (i.e., food, housing, health care, etc.), better access to education, more resources, and more connections to people who hold wealth and power than children who are raised in households with income levels below the federal poverty line. That seems pretty obvious.

On the opposite end of the socioeconomic spectrum we find failing schools, lack of educational opportunities, insufficient resources, food insecurity, lack of consistent housing, higher levels of crime, lack of access to higher education, lack of job opportunities . . . the list goes on and on. And that doesn't even consider the impacts of racial disparity, discrimination, and systemic bias that are significant barriers in the lives of people of color and people from historically underrepresented backgrounds.

The brutal but honest truth is that one who lacks wealth and privilege may not have an attainable chance of success regardless of the grit factor, depending on what other impediments exist. Some systemic barriers and external factors simply cannot be overcome by grit alone, at least not for many people.

A real-world comparison

Let's make this comparison a little more concrete. Let's consider two real people—two college students whom I personally know.

The first let's call Alexis (not her real name). Alexis is a white female whose father started a small business decades ago that, over time, grew to be a pretty big business. She had the privilege of attending the most exclusive, expensive private high school in her state. It is the kind of place that has a headmaster rather than a principal, a campus that resembles that of a small private college, small class sizes, classrooms outfitted with cutting-edge technology, and tuition starting at $20,000 per year for *kindergarten*.[5]

Alexis was a good student who earned good grades. She had the benefit of personal attention from teachers, an attentive mom who helped her with homework, and access to private tutors when needed. Unlike many teenagers, Alexis didn't have a part-time job. She didn't play any sports. She wasn't involved in theater or choir, and she didn't play any musical instruments. She studied enough to do well academically. She did what was expected of her. But she never went above and beyond. In short, in my humble opinion as an outsider looking in, Alexis lacked grit.

During her high school years, Alexis's parents hired a "college coach" to guide her through everything from course selection in ninth grade through the editing of essays for her college applications. A year before she sat for the ACT exam, her parents enrolled her in an ACT prep course and then hired a tutor to help her brush up on her weaker subjects. All of this—the prestigious high school, the tutors, the prep courses, the college coach—was enough to land Alexis a spot at the highly competitive, flagship public school in her state. Alexis continued on the same path during her college years. Good grades. No sports or academic clubs. She did land a competitive internship at a prestigious company where, maybe not coincidentally, one of the senior executives is her father's friend. On paper, Alexis looks very successful: good grades at a flagship university with a great internship on her resume. Not class valedictorian, but far better than average.

In contrast, let me tell you about Kamila (also not her real name). Kamila and her family immigrated to the United States when she was in elementary school. At that time, no one in Kamila's family spoke English. She was placed in a standard classroom in an inner-city school in a large public school district. Other than the English language learning teacher who spent some time in Kamila's classroom (and who spoke only English and Spanish, neither of which Kamila spoke), the school district provided no extra resources to help Kamila.

Her parents worked part-time jobs in addition to their full-time jobs. Kamila was responsible for taking care of her younger siblings after school until she, too, was old enough to earn a paycheck. In the school district she attended, the graduation rate hovers around 65 percent depending on the year (said differently, roughly a third of the students never finish high school). Over 90 percent of the students in the district are students of color, and over 75 percent fall into the "economically disadvantaged" category per the United States Department of Education.[6]

Despite these challenges, Kamila not only learned to speak and write the English language fluently, but she excelled at it. She rose from an elementary school student who did not speak English to become a state champion in high school debate. When it came time to take the ACT exam, she bought a study guide on Amazon. Money was needed for things like food and rent. The idea of paying for an ACT prep course was not even up for discussion.

While her ACT scores and high school record would have been competitive at the same flagship public university that Alexis attended, Kamila didn't even apply. Instead, she enrolled at the lesser known and much lower ranked local public college. Attending the flagship university would have required her to move several hours away. Money was tight, but the family always figured out a solution. For Kamila, that meant living with her parents, working, and attending the closest, least expensive college. She was grateful to even have the opportunity to attend college, as that was far out of reach for her parents a generation prior.

For the next few years, Kamila lived at home with her parents while she worked full time and took a full-time college course load. She continued to help care for her younger siblings as much as she could. In her very limited free time, Kamila led a mentoring group for students of color at her college. Despite the heavy workload plus her academic load, despite her family obligations, and despite every other challenge that came her way, Kamila earned grades that routinely placed her on the dean's list.

By the time I met Kamila, she was well into her third year of college, and she was on-track for graduation. While working full time and taking courses year round, Kamila completed her bachelor's degree, with honors, in four years. I told her how extraordinary her accomplishments were, and how incredibly impressed I was with her ability to complete her college degree while working a full-time job. She didn't think she was particularly noteworthy or extraordinary. To her, she simply did what was required in order to achieve her goal of attaining a college degree. To me, this is the definition of a young woman with a tremendous amount of grit. Kamila has grit with a capital G.

One out of every three students in Kamila's high school class did not make it to their high school graduation. Only a small percentage attended a four-year university. Even fewer completed their college degrees. The barriers are just too great for many of the students in Kamila's neighborhood and socioeconomic class.

Simply put, the starting lines for these two individuals were not equal. The finish line was not the same. The race was not fair. Not even close. Alexis had the best education, private tutors, prep courses, and the freedom to spend as much time as she needed or wanted on her studies. Kamila, by contrast, had enormous obstacles to overcome.

Grit is a factor, to be sure. But it is just one factor of many.

What are we missing when we focus on grit?

I argue that grit is not the most important factor to success. In certain situations, grit may even be used as an excuse.

Consciously or subconsciously, grit can be used as an excuse that allows people in positions of power to ignore, overlook, or downplay underlying issues in their organizations. By focusing on grit, attention is turned away from critical underlying problems like cultural bias, systemic bias, inequity, inequality, and other barriers to success. Leaders can use (intentionally or subconsciously) a "lack of grit" as the reason why some people (namely women, people of color, and people who identify as LGBTQIA+) do not rise to higher levels or achieve greater success.

Said differently, the focus on grit allows those in positions of power the grace of not having to take a very hard look at their own organizations to determine what else might be going on. If given the choice between acknowledging inherent inequality or attributing someone's lack of success to a lack of grit, isn't it easier and less painful for the organization to shift the focus to the individual who isn't rising to the top?

If we as a society consider grit to be the critical factor to success, then we don't have to admit the cards are stacked against women (or people of color, or people of historically disadvantaged backgrounds, or people who identify as LGBTQIA+, or people who were raised in a lower socioeconomic class). In other words, maybe it isn't the organization's fault. Maybe it is the women's fault. If women only possessed enough grit, women would succeed in equal numbers to men.

Telling people they lack grit places the focus on the individual, rather than on the institutional or systemic barriers. And if we focus enough on our own shortcomings, maybe we won't look at the other factors, biases, inequities, and barriers that impede our success.

Hopefully I haven't lost you already. Before you dismiss my thoughts as radical, overly reactionary, defensive, anti-intellectual, or otherwise, please hear me out. Please read on.

Systemic barriers

In 1987, the American Bar Association (ABA) established a Commission on Women in the Profession to "assess the status of women in the legal profession, identify barriers to advancement, and to recommend to the ABA actions to address problems identified." Under the leadership of Hillary Rodham Clinton, the Commission's early work concluded that women were not advancing within the legal profession at a satisfactory rate. The Commission found that a "variety of discriminatory barriers" existed within the professional culture as a whole. Even a significant increase in the number of women lawyers would not change the outcomes for women in general. Women alone would not be able to eliminate the systemic barriers, the Commission concluded. The Commission called for "a thorough reexamination of the attitudes and structures" in the legal profession.[7]

In other words, the Commission concluded that the problem was not with the women themselves, nor could it be solved by the women themselves. The problem was with the system. The system needed to change. Women were not to blame for their lack of success and advancement. The Commission recognized it was the culture, the systems, and the institutions that were holding women back. Until those things changed, we could not possibly expect women as a whole to make significant progress in the working world.

The year 1987 was a very long time ago. At the time Hillary Rodham Clinton led the Commission, she was still the First Lady of Arkansas. She had not yet ascended to the White House, the United States Senate, or the Democratic Party nomination for president. Yes, much time has passed since 1987.

Decades later, yet little progress

I wish I could say the 1987-era conclusions are no longer relevant. But that would not be correct. Much remains the same even today. Over thirty-five years later, the Commission on Women in the Legal Profession still exists. Such little progress has been made in the last three and a half decades that the ABA continues to convene the

Commission's work. And the Commission continues to study why women have not made significant enough inroads in the workplace.

Think of how entirely different our world is today as compared to thirty-five years ago. The internet. Mobile phones. Facebook, Netflix, Google, Amazon, YouTube. Alexa. GPS. Things we use and rely on every single day—none of those things existed in 1987. Our cutting-edge technology back then was a VHS tape. DVDs would not even be invented for another seven years. (And when was the last time you even saw a DVD?) We took pictures on analog cameras and then brought the rolls of film to a retail store to be developed. We drove in cars with terrestrial radio and windows we had to roll down manually. If we were really lucky, rudimentary cable television was available in our neighborhood. Otherwise, we watched nothing but the local channels and the VHS tapes we rented from Blockbuster, if we were lucky enough to live in a city that had one of the first Blockbuster locations. We got our news from newspapers that were delivered to our houses each morning. If we wanted to know the weather forecast, we picked up a landline and called a phone number. Our entire household shared one phone number, and we had no idea who was calling when the phone rang. It might be our father's boss, or our mother's sister, or our sister's boyfriend, or our best friend. And if you lived in a house with multiple teenagers like I did, the arguments over who got to use the one phone line were epic.

No, dinosaurs weren't walking the Earth in 1987. But it was a drastically different world. If, as a society, we were able to invent all of these life-changing things that today we cannot exist without, why haven't we been able to make a noticeable improvement in the advancement of women in the workplace? Why are women still fighting this battle?

Think about it. It's about priorities. Cultures. Institutions. Systems. Power.

Over three decades later, the same types of barriers to women advancing in the professional world remain. We haven't solved the problems. We haven't even made huge progress. Even more concerning (at least to me), the ABA has shifted focus away from examining the systemic problems or the discriminatory barriers to advancement and is blaming instead a "lack of grit."

The Grit Project

In recent years, the Commission turned its focus away from examining the "discriminatory barriers"[8] that prevent women from achieving equality in the workplace. Instead, they turned to studying individual traits that contributed to the success of women who held senior leadership roles. Said differently, it appears the Commission no longer views the lack of equality as a societal or structural problem that must be addressed at a systemic level. Instead, they now focus on the personality characteristics (and deficiencies) of the women themselves, with the aim of helping women build the characteristics that are common among those who succeeded in reaching higher levels of success.

Let's dig into the details. In 2012, the Commission conducted a study to identify the common characteristics of women who held senior-level positions. The study identified key traits that were common among these highly successful women. Those traits are described as "grit" and "the growth mindset." The Commission found a "statistically significant relationship between grit and success for women."[9]

"Alarmed by persistent evidence" that women are still failing to rise to senior-level positions in adequate numbers, the Commission formalized its work into a new initiative.[10] This initiative is called the Grit Project. The purpose of the Grit Project is to educate women about "the science behind grit and growth mindset." The Commission found that grit and having a growth mindset are important traits that many successful women have in common.[11] The Commission reasoned that more women can achieve success if they can increase their grittiness, if you will.

Notice the singular focus on women. Certainly, there must be some men who lack grit. There must be some men who could benefit from the Grit Project. Or are we to assume that men are doing fine just as they are, and only the female population has a problem with a lack of grit?

The Commission seems to be saying the problem is not with the institutions, systems, or cultures, or with the existence of discrimination or other barriers. The problem is not systemic, and therefore it does not require a broader solution. Instead, the Commission is saying (many? most?) women lack sufficient grit to succeed. It makes sense then, that if we can teach women how to increase their level of grit, then more women will be able to achieve greater success in the workplace. At least that's the theory.

The Commission created an entire website for the Grit Project where it houses various resources intended to teach women about grit and the growth mindset.[12] It includes a "21 Day Grit and Growth Mindset Challenge" which offers daily exercises composed of activities, articles, videos, and case studies that are intended to help women acquire tools to develop grit.[13] The challenge asks women to complete self-assessments, watch TED Talks, listen to podcasts, and read blog posts and academic articles written by thought leaders.

I don't have any issue with the material itself; in fact, the works of some of my favorite podcasters and thought leaders (I'm talking about you, Brené Brown) are included in the materials. My issue with all of this is its underlying message, its failure to address the larger problems, and its overtone of placing the blame and the burden of change on the shoulders of women themselves.

My rebuttal

Instead of focusing on the previously found discriminatory barriers that inhibit the success of women, the Commission instead turned its focus to individual personality characteristics. Ignore the universal. Focus on the individual. The key to success, in their view, is to increase one's grit level. The converse message is this: if you aren't successful, that must mean there is something deficient within your own character. It isn't that the world or the workplace is unfairly stacked against you; the problem is YOU.

To me, this feels a lot like blaming the women.

The Grit Project sends the message that it is a woman's inability or unwillingness to put forth the necessary effort that leads to her lack of success. It tells us we can improve our situation if we put in the effort and do the work to improve ourselves.

This feels like the Commission is telling me the problem is ME, not the institutions that set the rules of the game. The problem isn't that I am treated differently, discriminated against, not given equal opportunities, not viewed as equal by my boss or my peers, that I've had to endure some pretty disgusting and harassing behavior, or the multitude of other inequalities so many of us have experienced. They want the problem to be with the women. And, to be blunt, that's bullshit.

I could tell countless stories about the biases I've endured, both big and small. I'm not unique by any means. I think most women I know in the corporate world have similar stories to tell. The off-color jokes. The sexist comments. The staring at my boobs. The invitations to golf that went to all the guys on my team but none of the women. The statement that we should "bring our dollar bills for the evening entertainment" which was said from the stage of an all-company meeting. The weekly guys' lunches I was never invited to. The constant mistaking me for someone's assistant rather than the person in charge. The handing down of client relationships based on what can only be described as the old boys' club culture. The snide comments made behind the backs of my female colleagues when they had family obligations to attend to. The jokes about my friends being on a "three-month vacation" when they took maternity leave. The examples are everywhere.

No amount of "21 Day Challenges" will change any of that.

Call out the real problem

Where do we go from here?

I don't know. I don't have the answers. But I do know the problem is NOT with you. No amount of grit on your part will level the playing field, fix the biases, or remove the barriers.

Think back to my story about Alexis and Kamila, the college students who came from two very different worlds. Kamila has more grit than possibly anyone I've ever met in my life (and I've met some really tough people). No amount of grit on her part could ever equal the playing field for her. She was dealt a life that included under-funded and underperforming schools, lack of opportunities, lack of resources, and socioeconomic struggles. Through her incredible determination and hard work, she attained her college degree. But admittedly, her resume does not match that of the privileged Alexis. Alexis attended a higher-ranked flagship university and landed a prestigious internship, two things Kamila had no way of doing regardless of grit. Sometimes it is the system—not the person—that needs to change.

We need to stop blaming the women. We need to stop telling women and young girls that the problem is with THEM. We need to recognize that life is not fair. Everyone does not begin the race at the same starting line. For some people, the race starts far, far behind and it takes everything they have just to try to catch up. Some people have far more hurdles and obstacles to overcome than others. And for some, those hurdles and obstacles are simply too numerous, too high, and impossible to clear.

We need to call out the biases. Refuse to stand for discriminatory behavior when we encounter it. We need to speak up and speak out. Loudly. Stand together and tell the world we will not be blamed. We need to rail against studies such as the Grit Project.

Maybe most importantly, we need to help one another. Support each other. Lend a hand. Be a mentor. Champion each other's successes. Use your platform and your voice to lift up other women. Create the kind of culture for the next generation that we wished we had for ourselves.

Those who hold some of the power have the best platform for making their voices heard. For creating change. I know I come from a place of great privilege. I have white privilege, economic privilege, educational privilege, cultural privilege, the free time to consider these things, and the space to make my voice heard. I'm done working in the corporate world. I don't have to worry about possible career implications if I cause some trouble or piss off some people. So that's what I am going to keep doing.

I want the world to be a better place for the people I've dedicated this book to, and for all the younger women who read it (and those who don't). Someday I want them to look back at my stories and think of them with the same relief I have when I watch *Mad Men*— thank God the world isn't like that anymore.

Until then, I'll keep writing and talking and calling out the wrongs that I see. I will keep treading loudly. And I hope you will, too.

KEY TAKEAWAYS

- Having grit is important, but be careful how much emphasis is placed on it. It is just one of many factors that contribute to success.

- No amount of grit will level the playing field, eliminate the biases, or remove the barriers to women's success in the corporate world.

- Don't let anyone tell you that your lack of grit is what is holding you back. Sometimes it is the system—not the person—that needs to change.

- Let's promise to help each other out, champion one another's successes, and use our platforms and our voices to lift one another up.

10

Quitting Is Not Failure

If you are one of those people who has that little voice
in the back of her mind saying, "Maybe I could do [fill in
the blank]," don't tell it to be quiet. Give it a little room to
grow, and try to find an environment it can grow in.

—REESE WITHERSPOON[1]

Twenty years. That's how long it took for me to get from the first day of kindergarten to the first day of my first "real job." Thirteen years of elementary school, middle school, and high school. Four years of college. Three years of law school. Two summer internships. A few job offers before graduation day. Then finally, at twenty-five years old, I made it there. To my dream job.

It was the goal I had worked toward for all those years. The job that would make my parents proud to tell their friends where their daughter had landed. The one that would pay off my student loan debt ahead of schedule. The one that would boost my resume. The one that would prove to the world—and to myself—that I had achieved something. All of that would make me happy. . . Wouldn't it?

To be honest, I never thought about the possibility there might not be a life of happiness at the end of the rainbow. Or that there might not even *be* an end to the rainbow. I'd followed the path laid out for me into corporate life without questioning anything. Follow the rules, do what you are told, check each box, and move to the next square. That, I believed, would lead to a successful career and a happy life. That is what I was told—by my teachers, by my parents, and by society—and I never questioned it.

What if your dream job isn't a dream?

A funny thing happened on my way to the promised life: That first job wasn't a dream. No job is a dream job, at least not in my experience. It was reality, and it was far from perfect. It was a shit ton of work. It was a lot of pressure. The hours were long, and the expectations were high. The atmosphere was competitive, to put it nicely.

In the first year, I developed terrible headaches and a not-very-cute eye twitch. Then came the stomachaches, the crying (sometimes for no reason other than just feeling overwhelmed), and the occasional meltdown. Later came the lectures from my doctor about stress and high blood pressure. Maybe I was not cut out for this life, I thought. But I was hell-bent on proving to the world that I was entirely cut out for it.

To make matters worse, I felt like a fraud. I felt like I knew nothing about the work I was supposed to be doing. I thought it would only be a matter of time before someone realized I was bluffing my way through each day. It was not just a newbie feeling that went away quickly. I felt this way *for years*.

I didn't have the vocabulary or insight into others' experiences back then to know what I was feeling was a pretty common case of Imposter Syndrome, a phenomenon far too many women experience in their careers. No one talked about any of this, at least not in my universe. Social media didn't exist yet, and there were no conversations in traditional media or in the world around us discussing the struggles young women face in corporate America. It felt like we were out there on our own, in an environment where most of our colleagues would never admit to feeling any of this. Of course, then, I assumed I was the only one who felt that way.

With the long hours, the pressure, and the constant feeling of insecurity, my first job wasn't a dream at all. It was a *job*. And I was struggling. Looking back, it wasn't the right workplace culture for me. That's on me. I chose that company. I now know I would have been happier in a workplace culture that was more nurturing, collaborative, and supportive. Yes, I had an assigned mentor (the word "assigned" being the operative part of that sentence). In the first six months of my career, I could have counted on one hand the total number of times I spoke to, saw, or had any communication with my assigned mentor. Had I totaled up every interaction, it amounted to maybe fifteen minutes of his time over all those months.

It was a sink-or-swim culture and I felt like I was plummeting to the bottom of the ocean. Fast. Instead of cutting my losses and quitting right away, though, I stayed. And stayed. I figured some things out, made some changes, then stayed even longer.

Maybe it will get better

It's pretty easy to understand why most people, myself included, don't quit the jobs they kind of hate right away. You have to give it a chance. You have to figure out what you're doing before you can judge the company or the job itself. You can't give up so easily. You worry about the implications on your resume. You worry what other people will think. Also, there's a little thing called money. You have rent due, car payments, student loans, credit card bills . . . the list goes on and on. You put your head down, you go to the job you kind of hate, and you hope it becomes more tolerable over time. Maybe you will even learn to love it, once you figure out what the hell it is you're meant to be doing. That was my great hope. I stayed, and stayed, waiting for it all to get better.

It did get better in a lot of ways. I really liked the people I worked with. I found a real mentor, someone who took immense amounts of time and patience to teach me everything I know. The Imposter Syndrome lessened. I learned a ton. I got better at doing my actual job. And I settled in.

There were periods when it was tolerable, even pretty good. There were times when it was actually fun. I always felt pride in where I worked. But even in the good times, I couldn't shake the feeling of dread. I dreaded driving to work more days than not. I dreaded the Sunday night feeling of another work week looming ahead. I dreaded the long hours and the high pressure. I dreaded having to cancel week-end plans (often) because a client or a senior-level person dropped work on me on Friday afternoon and needed it done by Monday. I resented the three years in a row that I was in the office on Christmas Eve day. I resented every Mother's Day, Father's Day, Memorial Day, July Fourth, and Labor Day that I spent working. I resented every postponed or canceled vacation. I resented that work consumed my life. But that was the life that I chose. What right did I have to be so disappointed with how life was turning out for me? And if I was so unhappy, why didn't I just leave?

What if it doesn't get better?

What do you do if, after a while, you still kind of hate your job? I'm not saying you have to love your job or be that unicorn of a person who would rather work on a Saturday instead of settling in for a good Netflix binge. I'm talking about the rest of us. What if you think you'd be happier at another company? Or in another industry or profession? Or what if you find yourself in a work environment that is hostile, harassing, or even straight-up toxic?

How do you know if the situation you're in is only a temporary rough spot or if you should quit? When do the warning signs pile up high enough that you finally realize quitting is the only answer? And, probably most importantly, why do we tend to delay quitting a job that is making us unhappy? Those, my friends, are very complicated questions. I don't have all the answers. But I'll try to explain what I've come to know over the course of a few jobs that I should have quit long before I actually did so.

Why do we stay?

By the time I finally quit a few of the companies I've worked for, I was burned out, stressed out, and worn down. There were enough reasons for me to leave each job long before I did. I stayed. And stayed. And stayed some more, until I literally felt I had no other option but to quit. Looking back, I realize now I should have stopped trying to force myself to stay.

I don't think my experience is unusual, though. I've seen this more times than I care to acknowledge. I know too many women—successful, intelligent women—who stay in jobs they kind of hate (or really hate) for far longer than is healthy or necessary. Why do we do this to ourselves?

That, my friends, is the million-dollar question with a very complex answer.

Learned behaviors stay with us

In elementary school, I was the kid who studied hard to win the spelling bee, who had to be in the highest reading group, and who wanted to be the teacher's favorite. When my third-grade teacher had us read aloud in class, I would count out the kids ahead of me and the paragraphs of the book, then silently practice my paragraph so I could almost recite it from memory when my turn came. I actually liked parent-teacher conferences. Sometimes I would ask my mom if I could come along. There was nothing better in my nine-year-old mind than hearing my teacher say, "Kristine is a pleasure to have in class."

Yep, I was *that kid*. I think a lot of women (or at least the women I know) are that kid. We, as young girls, were conditioned from a very early age to seek the approval of others. So that's what we did.

Thinking back on this now, that kid needed to care less about what others thought of her. That kid needed to be told winning isn't everything. That kid needed to learn that external praise does not result in internal happiness. Had any of that happened, maybe I wouldn't have found quitting a job I didn't like to be such a struggle. Maybe I didn't quit so many things in life sooner because I was afraid of disappointing someone.

Maybe some of this is inherent in my soul. Maybe it was drilled into me by my parents, my coaches, and my teachers. Back in the 1980s of my youth, not everyone got a trophy. Not everyone got praised. We weren't told we were unique or special. More often than not, we were told the opposite. We were told there was nothing particularly special about us so we better work harder. Not everyone won. And I wanted to win.

Growing up, my dad would often say, "I don't care if you sweep floors for a living as long as you are the best floor sweeper in the world." Notice he didn't say, "I don't care what you do, as long as you *do your best.*" He said, "as long as you *are the best.*" Thinking back now and considering his advice in the totality of his life experience, I don't think my dad was demanding perfection. I don't think he meant I would never be good enough unless I was the ultimate winner. I think he was demanding that I work my ass off, stay dedicated, and take pride in whatever it was that I chose to do. My dad came from a pretty humble upbringing. He was raised in the aftermath of World War II by parents who survived wars, the Great Depression, and a sometimes-heavy dose of discrimination. Being an Eastern European immigrant did not make one super popular in those days. By the time I was maybe ten years old, I think I'd heard every Polish joke known to humankind, and they were not kind to my people. I can only imagine what my grandparents experienced half a century prior. Nonetheless, my grandparents were extremely proud, hardworking, working-class people. They didn't have much, but they were very proud of what they did have. They instilled those beliefs in my dad who, in turn, instilled them in me. Work as hard as you can. Be proud. Hold your head high. Endure. Push through. And be the best at whatever situation in life you find yourself in.

Not surprisingly, my gymnastics coaches had a very similar outlook. Don't just work hard. Work harder than everyone else. Be laser-focused on your goals. Push through the pain and the tough times. And *be the best.* After all, there is only one gold medal and only two other spots on the podium. It was just like at the Olympics, except this was middle America, I was a child, and I was not an elite-level athlete. But that didn't matter. All I heard was this message: Grind through it, hold your head high, work harder than everyone else, don't let anyone throw you off course, and be the best. I'm sure I'm not the only one who had these kinds of experiences. Take any sport, any competition, any game and you'll find similar themes and messages. We constantly teach children that hard work pays off, that perseverance is a virtue, and that they have to "stick with it" to come out on top.

While the movie *Talladega Nights* wouldn't be released for another two decades, it's as if my dad and my gymnastics coaches were preaching the infamous words of Ricky Bobby: "If you ain't first, you're last."[2]

Added on top of all of that are the messages we heard (consciously and subconsciously) as little girls and, in many ways, the messages we continue to hear as women. Little girls are conditioned by society from a very young age to behave in a certain way. We are taught to be people pleasers. We are conditioned to be caretakers. We learn to seek praise and approval from others. We are told to be good girls. We are taught to not make a fuss. We are told that girls shouldn't demand things. We are conditioned to be accommodating.

Look at most Disney (and non-Disney) movies marketed for children, look at most children's cartoons and books, or look at most mainstream movies and television shows even today. If you pay attention, you'll be able to read the messages to women and little girls loud and clear: Be nice. Be a good girl. Don't cause a fuss. Smile. Be quiet. Be likeable. Be the object of desire. You're weaker and vulnerable, and you need to be saved. Wait for your prince to come.

I'm no scientist, therapist, or expert of any kind. But I know myself pretty well. And I know those messages from childhood stayed buried within me. Whether we realize it or not, the messages we heard even as ten-year-olds impact us in our careers and our adult lives. They shape our beliefs of ourselves. They help form our personality, our work ethic, our grit, our values, and even our actions.

Think back to my twenty-year progression. Twenty years of being educated, taught, and groomed for the future. Twenty years of working for the A grades, thinking I had to make the honor roll, win the awards, and get the acceptance letter that would grant me access to the next level.

Twenty years of being told that hard work pays off. Twenty years of following every rule and doing everything the "right" way (academically, I mean . . . I did break more than my share of other kinds of rules in my high school and college years, but that's a topic for another book that I will never write). Twenty years of believing there was only one path to success. Twenty years of chasing the end of the rainbow. Twenty long years, all so I could have what I thought would be a dream career.

If I quit any particular company, I would be admitting that my job—and by extension my life—was anything but a dream. Even worse, I was afraid I would be viewed as a failure. There's a certain mentality that permeates work culture: the idea that the people who quit are the ones who don't have what it takes to be successful. In some corporate cultures, quitting is viewed as an admission of defeat, of inferiority. That was absolutely the case at several companies where I've worked. We (myself included for many years) viewed people who quit as people who couldn't cut it, weren't good enough at their jobs, or weren't going to be promoted. So they quit. I now know just how wrong this is, but this was a common view at several stops along my career path.

Quitting is not failure

The truth is that sometimes quitting is the right answer. Sometimes quitting is success. It is refusing to work in a corporate culture, career, or particular job that doesn't fit you, your goals, or your life. In some cases, it is refusing to tolerate hostile or toxic behavior. In others, it is refusing to stay in a situation that doesn't fulfill you. It is putting yourself, your family, your well-being, and your priorities first. It is saying, "I know this job/company/culture/environment isn't for me, and I value myself enough to prioritize my happiness and well-being over this."

Trust yourself. Trust your instincts. If you think you may want to quit your job, your company, your career, or anything else in life, lean into that feeling. It is coming from somewhere and it's trying to tell you something very important. Don't dismiss it. Don't waste your time trying to make a wrong-fitting culture, particular job, or career work for you. It is okay to leave if you don't feel fulfilled. It is more than okay. By staying, you are actually preventing yourself from finding the place where you will be happiest. Staying may be preventing you from future success elsewhere.

We have the power to change our own lives. As women, we often stay too long in jobs, workplaces, and cultures that are not good for us, or not meeting our needs, or not healthy, or something we just don't want. We think quitting equals failure. This is particularly true of women who work in coveted positions or who work for very prestigious companies. We stay because the outside world views this job as prestigious, views us as successful, and envies something about our company, our position, or our lives. It's like the famous line from the movie *The Devil Wears Prada*: "A million girls would kill for this job."[3] It's an awful job. Yet we stay. We stay because it is the job that other people want.

Sometimes we stay even though we are unhappy, unfulfilled, or even miserable. We stay because we believe leaving means we will disappoint people. I, personally, stayed too long in jobs that didn't mesh with my priorities. That didn't fit my ideal life as I envisioned it. That I didn't love or even like. That weren't consistent with my goals and values. And in at least one case, I stayed too long at a place that made me feel unequal because of my gender. I stayed to the detriment of my mental health, my relationships, and my family. I thought I could change the system from the inside. I thought leaving would be viewed as failure. I stayed because, in the eyes of my profession, these were all "great" jobs. At some point, though, we need to realize when it is time to walk away. Sometimes walking away IS success.

I resisted walking away because I saw quitting as losing . . . as admitting defeat . . . until eventually I could not endure any more.

I want women today to trust themselves. To act on their instincts. To refuse to tolerate what I went through. To create the lives they want, and not stay in situations that don't serve them because society views those roles as prestigious or the job everyone else wants.

I want every woman to know it is absolutely okay—and not at all a sign of weakness—to walk away from any work environment that isn't right for you, that doesn't serve you, or that isn't the life you want. I want every woman to know that sometimes quitting is the best option. Sometimes quitting is not only what has to be done, but it is the definition of success.

KEY TAKEAWAYS

- Trust yourself. Listen to your inner voice. If you think it is time to quit your job, it probably is.

- Make decisions that will lead to the career and the life you really want, regardless of whether that's the career or life that society places high value on.

- If you are in a workplace culture that is inconsistent with your goals, values, or priorities, leave. And do it sooner rather than later.

- Don't waste time trying to make a wrong-fitting culture or a wrong-fitting career work for you. Some things just don't fit, and that's okay.

- Quitting is not failure. Sometimes quitting is the only way to achieve success in the long term.

11

Where Do We Go from Here?

I am inviting you to step forward, to be seen, and to
ask yourself: If not me, who? If now now, when?

—EMMA WATSON[1]

When I entered the working world over two decades ago,
I was filled with hope: Hope for my future and hope
that my gender would be irrelevant. The generations of
women who came before me had done the hardest work and paved
the path for me. We had reached critical mass, I assumed. Mindsets
had changed, I thought. Equality of all people (not just what we think
of as traditional gender equality but also equality of gender identity,
gender expression, sexual orientation, race, ethnicity, national origin,
religion, ability, age, and familial status) was within reach, I naïvely
believed. The most important and most difficult battles had already
been won by the generations who came before. There was not much
left to fight for . . . or so I thought.

The state of the world today

While much has changed in the last few decades, too much has remained the same. Only forty-four of the nation's 500 largest publicly traded corporations are headed by female CEOs.[2] That means more than nine out of every ten CEOs of Fortune 500 companies are men. To add to the astonishment, the current number of female CEOs is a record-breaking, smashing improvement. It was such a remarkable fact that *Fortune* chose to title its article "The Number of Women Running Fortune 500 Companies Reaches a Record High." Breaking records is great. Breaking records makes for nice headlines. But the simple truth remains, and it bears repeating. Over 90 percent of the largest publicly traded companies in the United States are led by men.

Shifting to the business world outside of the Fortune 500, the numbers are better but not dramatically so. Women comprise only about one in four C-suite-level positions in corporate America. We aren't just talking about companies with female CEOs. We are talking about women in senior leadership roles across a broad cross-section of businesses of varying sizes, revenues, numbers of employees, industries, business sectors, products, services, geographic locations, and public and private companies.[3]

Looking at the entrepreneurial side of business, the data is both encouraging and stunningly bad. On the bright side, female-owned businesses generate a staggering $1.8 trillion in revenue per year in the United States.[4] To get an idea of how big that number is, one trillion equals 1000 billion. It's hard to conceptualize . . . but let's try anyway. If you started counting right now, one number per second, it would take you over thirty-one years to reach one billion. If you kept counting to one trillion, it would take over 31,000 years. Now multiply that by 1.8. That is how much revenue is generated by female-owned businesses in the United States each year.

Despite that massive dollar amount, female entrepreneurs and business owners face an uphill battle. This is particularly true when it comes to raising funds to start or grow their businesses. For example, in 2019 (the most recent year for which data is available), just 2.7 percent of all venture capital dollars went to female-founded companies.[5] Said differently, more than ninety-seven cents of every dollar invested by venture capital firms went to businesses founded by men. The disparities between companies run or owned by men versus those run or owned by women are too stark to ignore, and the impacts are obvious in every category from the largest of the Fortune 500 companies to the smallest of start-ups. We have a very, very long way to go before women reach equality in leadership/CEO positions and in investment in their businesses.

Shifting to the government realm, things aren't much better. After 231 years and a string of 48 white men, Vice President Kamala Harris made history in 2021. Finally, someone other than a man sits in the White House. Of course, we've yet to have a female president.

Of the 535 members of the United States Congress, as of January 2023, only 153 are women. Women comprising just over one-quarter of Congress was record-breaking, headline-making stuff. It was lauded as "the highest percentage in U.S. history and a considerable increase from where things stood even a decade ago."[6] Progress is great. Progress should be lauded. But the raw fact remains: women still account for just over one out of every four members of Congress, the legislative body that is intended to represent the people of this country, over half of whom are women (per the United States Census Bureau[7]).

Only twelve of the fifty states are led by a female governor.[8] This number is up from just nine in the prior election cycle, which tied the number of female governors originally set back in 2004.[9] Said differently, from 2004 to 2020, this country made zero gain in electing even one additional female governor. The 2022 election was record-breaking in that it added three more women to the governor ranks. Breaking records is great. But why, almost 250 years after the founding of our country, is it still record-breaking to have over 75 percent of the states be led by men?

We should not be happy—or even satisfied—with this progress.

Gender inequality in the broader society

Considering these and similar statistics across industries and professions, it is difficult to deny that women still face an uphill battle in the professional world—and in the world in general. The reality is that gender inequality persists not only in the workplace but also in our greater society.

Perhaps more accurately, gender inequality persists in the workplace *because of* its pervasiveness in our society. In the view of some segment of our population, women are still viewed as inferior, or too emotional, or less intelligent, or less dedicated to our careers, or just objects to be desired. It is this mindset that must change, for until women are viewed as equal beings in our own right, we will never be treated as equal in the workplace.

The past half decade has been weird, to be sure (and I'm not even talking about the global pandemic and resulting two years in which many of us rarely left our homes). It was a less-than-stellar period for women, women's rights, and gender equality.

It was the period in which we saw sixty women accuse Bill Cosby, America's favorite TV dad, of sexual assault.[10] The early accusers were dismissed as liars, fame seekers, or gold diggers. But as the number of accusers grew and their stories sounded frighteningly similar, the truth was undeniable. While Cosby was eventually convicted of several felonies, he was released on a technicality after serving only three years in prison.[11] Today he is a free man.

It was also the time in which Brock Turner, a twenty-year-old scholarship athlete at Stanford University, was convicted of sexually assaulting an unconscious woman after a fraternity party. In asking for leniency, the perpetrator's father wrote a letter to the judge in which he stated that a jail sentence would be "a steep price to pay for 20 minutes of action."[12]

I don't know what bothers me the most: The fact that the perpetrator's father thought jail time was too harsh of a penalty for his son's criminal acts, or the fact that he characterized the sexual assault as "20 minutes of action." The perpetrator's punishment for committing this felony? He served a mere three months of jail time.[13] Today he is a free man.

This person was convicted of sexual assault by a jury of his peers. But he is not just any person. He is a white, economically advantaged, scholarship athlete at one of the most prestigious universities in the country. A felon. He served only three months in jail. Would that same sentence have been imposed on a man of a different race or ethnicity? Or a different socioeconomic class? Or if the felony had not been the sexual assault of a young woman of color, but a crime of a different nature? The issues raised by this case alone could fill an entire book. But I will leave that one for another author on another day.

The point is we should all feel incredibly uncomfortable with this story because it is not just a news story. It is a reflection of society. It is a sign that we need things to change. And, for things to change, someone has to make that change happen. The brave woman who was the victim of Brock Turner's criminal acts is helping make that happen. Her name is Chanel Miller, and you can read her story in her beautifully written book, *Know My Name: A Memoir*.[14] Resolved to not be defined by the felonies committed against her and the incredibly unfair result of the criminal trial, Chanel Miller continues to fight for change on college campuses and beyond through her advocacy, writing, art, and speaking engagements. In a world in need of more bravery, Chanel Miller is a pillar of strength.

Of course, we all also witnessed the tidal waves of the #MeToo and #TimesUp movements and the horrific truths that the brave victims came forward with about industry titans, CEOs, politicians, actors, producers, talk show hosts, musicians, music executives, church leaders, educators, financiers, professional athletes . . . the list goes on.

We all watched as television industry titan and former Fox News chairman Roger Ailes was sued for sexual harassment. Tens of thousands of workplace sexual harassment lawsuits are filed every year (a fact which, by itself, is sobering). What made this one unique was that more than twenty employees of a single workplace recounted numerous incidents of sexual harassment committed by the CEO of the company.[15] This cultural acceptance of the degradation of women persisted at Fox News for well over a decade. Ailes was ultimately removed from his post, but not before negotiating a $40 million payment from the network.[16] Let me say that again: a wealthy and powerful CEO who was accused of sexual harassment by numerous professional women for his behavior that persisted for more than a decade ended up leaving the company with a $40 million payout. How is this punishment?

This does not feel like progress to me. This does not sound like equality. Not even close. This cannot be our truth today. We cannot sit by and idly watch. It is time for us all to speak out.

Unequal in the eyes of the law

Over one hundred years after the Nineteenth Amendment to the United States Constitution was ratified, we are still writing about, talking about, and fighting for gender equality (not to mention equality of gender identity, gender expression, sexual orientation, race, ethnicity, national origin, religion, disability, age, and familial status, but those are topics for another day). We are still struggling to be viewed as equal. To be treated as equal. To BE equal.

One recent morning, I was feeling an unusual sense of desperation and despair. We knew the day was coming because a draft opinion of the United States Supreme Court had been leaked some six weeks prior. We knew the rights of women across the country were about to be turned back fifty years. We knew this in our heads. But in my heart, that day, June 24, 2022, still hit me in a way that is hard to describe. I never really, truly thought the day would come. I prayed Superman (in the form of Chief Justice Roberts) would somehow save us.

I didn't want to believe the laws of my country would no longer treat me as equal; that decisions about our bodily autonomy would lay in the hands of judges and legislators who had never met us. I didn't want to believe I would no longer have the same rights that men have to control their own bodies. This isn't about a single issue. This isn't just about reproductive rights. This isn't just about women's rights. This is about equality in the eyes of the law. This is about equality of all people.

If we are not equal in the eyes of the law, how can women ever be equal in the professional world? In the words of my personal hero, Justice Ruth Bader Ginsburg: "It is essential to woman's equality with man that she be the decisionmaker, that her choice be controlling . . . If you impose restraints that impede her choice, you are disadvantaging her because of her sex."[17]

As I lay in bed contemplating all that had happened in the last several years and all the possible future implications of the court decision, through the darkness came a (literal) ray of light. I noticed a text from my mom when I picked up my phone to silence the blue glow. My mother, a woman of the bra-burning era, a Gloria Steinem–loving, original feminist for equality. My mother, the matriarch of a family of three daughters, three granddaughters, one great-granddaughter, and a gay grandson. My mother, one of the smartest people I know despite the lack of educational opportunities possible for women of her generation or socioeconomic class.

In the words of this retired grandmother in her late seventies, I found hope. Strength. Inspiration. Pride. A duty to speak up. An obligation to speak out for all women and girls. A necessity to no longer remain quiet in the face of ongoing inequalities. An obligation to join the battle. A duty to speak what will be unpopular with some people who know me. A desire to fight for the young women and girls who come after me. A responsibility to fight for the next generation, just as those who came before me fought for my rights. I hope her words inspire some of you, too.

The text read:

> This does not mean we are done. Simply put, we must stand together and stand stronger. I know we can and we will. We women have been through worse. Maybe this was meant to be, hopefully opening the eyes and hearts of many. I know it has for me. It will be an uphill battle but it will be a battle worth fighting. Shoulder to the wheel and nose to the grindstone. Here we go again.

I choose hope

Today I choose hope. I choose to be inspired, even encouraged. I choose to be motivated. I choose to share stories from my life and my friends' lives, the humiliating parts and all, with the hope that our experiences will encourage, inspire, and comfort others.

I choose to say life is messy and difficult. I choose to admit I have struggled. To handle the stress, to find time to care for myself, to nurture relationships, to handle the adversity unfairly directed at me because of my gender, to eat what I should be eating instead of ordering pizza, and to sleep through the night without being haunted by the million things I need to do the next day. I've even struggled to find time to buy my own tampons. And that's okay. That's beautiful. That's real.

I choose action. I choose positivity. I choose to make a difference, if not for me, then for the next generation. I choose to highlight inequity and inequality, particularly in gender because that is what I know best. I choose to tell the truth, even the hard truths. Even if that means I lose some friends or family over it.

It might be the end of the world we once knew. But it is not the end. It is just the beginning. I invite you to join me. Shoulder to the wheel and nose to the grindstone. Here we go.

KEY TAKEAWAYS

- Women continue to be dramatically underrepresented in leadership roles of various types in America. From Fortune 500 CEOs, to senior leadership positions at a wide cross section of corporate America, to entrepreneurs receiving venture capital funding, to state governors, to representatives in Congress, the percentage of women continues to lag dramatically behind the percentage of men in these positions.

- There is much work to be done in the fight for gender equity and gender equality.

- I choose to be inspired. The fight for equality marches on.

Acknowledgments

This book was a journey that began with a series of blog posts in 2016. Thank you to Ms. JD, a nonprofit dedicated to the success of women lawyers, for giving me the opportunity and platform to create the blog and the confidence to believe my words could make a difference. In the year I spent as a writer in residence for Ms. JD, I found my voice and my purpose. My journey as a writer would never have happened had it not been for that experience.

My love and deepest gratitude to my husband, Kirk Larsen. You are my strength, my best friend, and my favorite person in the world. Your unconditional love, unwavering support, belief in me, and encouragement made all of this possible. You make everything in my life possible. You are my sine qua non.

Thank you to my family for your enduring love, support, and everything you've taught me. To my late father, Dewey Cherek, I miss you every day. You taught me the value of hard work and the virtue of earning my own way. Because of you, I strive to live my life honestly, ethically, with pride but not ego, and in a manner that honors our family name. To my mom, Donna Cherek, whose inspiring words are the closing of this book. You instilled in me the belief that I could do anything I wanted. Thank you for creating in me the values of equality, equity, and inclusion, and for inspiring me to fight for change. To my stepmom, Nan Gardetto, you showed me by example how a young woman can achieve great success in a business world dominated by men twice her age. You taught me to believe in myself, my abilities, and my vision. To my sister, Lisa Cherek, thank you for being the best role model and big sister I could've asked for. You took care of me, taught me, coached me, and paved the way for me in so many ways. I am forever grateful for all of you.

To Jackie Posselt and Kim Merbeth, you are the sisters of my soul and my biggest supporters. You encourage me, push me, and help me face the hard things. And, at some point during the long months of 2020 and 2021, you encouraged me to turn my restless energy toward something that would fill my spirit and intellect. That late-night FaceTime prompted me to dig out some old blog posts and see what I could turn them into. In addition to everything else I owe you in life, I owe you my eternal gratitude for inspiring me to put fingers to keyboard and begin writing.

To the Benetton Clan: Kathy Steinbauer, Sandy Merkel, Jill Budny, Jen Rauch, Jackie Posselt, and Kim Merbeth. For more than three decades you've stood by my side through the best of times and the worst. You are my conscience, voice of reason, and the ones who tell me what I need to hear (even when I don't want to hear it). You are the people I celebrate with, laugh with, cry with, and get through life with. Through it all, it has always been us, together.

To my dear friends Jen Rupkey, Amy Neurauter, and Jen Paluch. You've been my teammates, the people I cheered with, lived life with, traveled with, cried with, laughed with, and broke a few rules with. You encourage me, support me, challenge me, and inspire me. You've been by my side on my worst days and my best. I am so thankful for you.

Marti Wronski, thank you for being you. And thank you for letting me share with the world the story of our friendship. I always know you are right beside me, supporting me, encouraging me, and celebrating with me. And I with you. I couldn't have done life without you.

To Jessie Lochmann Allen, your suggestion all those years ago that I turn the blog posts into a book made me believe I could actually do it. Thank you for being my dear friend and for being the spark that ignited my dream to bring this book to reality.

To my incredible girlfriends who allowed me to share their (embarrassing) stories in this book, you mean the world to me. Thank you for helping me help the next generation.

To the teachers, coaches, friends, and colleagues who have, in various ways, played an important role in my life, thank you from the bottom of my heart. My sixth-grade teacher, Mrs. Alice Keough. My gymnastics coaches Lon Arfsten, Larry Pattis, Jeanelle Memmel, and Andy Memmel. My high school and college cheerleading coaches Jenny Peelen Thomas and Jane Vinson-Kafura. My colleagues at Foley & Lardner, especially Jessie Lochmann Allen, Leah Krider Gorham, Joe Rupkey, Tambre Ruud, and the Honorable Brett Ludwig who made my work days so much brighter; and Shelly Hart, Beth Corey, and Hugh O'Halloran who taught me everything I know (law-wise). My colleagues at Godfrey & Kahn, especially Nic Wahl for believing in me and always having faith in me. Professor Wenona Whitfield, who took me under her wing and taught me how to be a professor. Amanda Reid Payne and Caroline Nichols, who made my law school teaching years indescribably more enjoyable.

To the New Berlin Eisenhower cheerleaders I had the pleasure of coaching in the 2000s, you taught me more than I ever could have hoped to teach you. You made a lasting impression on my life through your dedication, hard work, teamwork, sacrifice, ability to persevere, tenacity, and your ability to push through demanding tumbling and stunts after being kicked in the head, hit in the face, nose bleeds running down your uniforms, nervous stomachs that sometimes caused a run to the bathroom to vomit minutes before you took the mat, and a judging scandal that almost left you out of the final round of Nationals . . . until you took the mat and won the whole damn National title. If anyone ever doubts the mental strength or toughness of a teenage girl, they've never met a competitive cheerleader. I am eternally grateful I had the opportunity to be part of each of your lives: Julia Moriwaki, Amber (Wilke) McKenzie, Brittany (Hasseldeck) Rick, Ashley Schroeder, Serena Maruko, Maggie (Tarnowski) Peake, Alysia Richards, Nicole Vollriede, Kristin Kohls, Sara (Duncan) O'Kimosh, Courtney (Nichols) Van Vooren, Amanda Laabs, Lacey Van Syckle, Staci (Garlock) Foy, Jamie (Mahn) O'Connell, Kelly Chiovatero, Nikki (Ergen) Markowski, Amy (Chmielewski) Stout, Stephanie (Schwamb) Dellis, Megan Wlodarski, Emilie (Poehlmann) Poulakos, Rachel Schlass, Bri (Izzo) Wussow, Allie (Jaques) Mayenschein, Lauren Rush, Emily (Bauman) Porcaro, Amanda Boettcher, Stephanie Contrucci, Stacey Kyne, Morgan Belongia, and Katelyn Hansmann.

A special thank you to Edlyn Biscocho and Angie (Nikolas) Emrey, the best co-coaches I could have asked for. And to all of the parents who gave me their unending support, belief, faith, and trust, thank you for sharing your daughters with me. To the entire IKE cheer family, I treasure our years together. IKE Cheer for Life!

Bringing a book to life takes the effort of a tremendous team. I found that team at Greenleaf Book Group. Thank you to everyone at Greenleaf for taking a chance on *Tread Loudly* and working so hard to bring it to life. My deepest gratitude to David Endris, Erin Brown, Lindsay Bohls, Killian Piraro, Sheila Parr, Valerie Howard, Amanda Marquette, Danielle Green, and Kayleigh Lovvorn. And my eternal gratitude to my editors Lindsey Clark and Tenyia Lee, who spent months painstakingly pouring over every word I had written, then sprinkled their magic to help me create something so much better. I could not have done this without all of you. You all have been true partners, advisers, teachers, and guides throughout the process.

Thank you to the team at BrainTrust for believing in this book. I am honored and grateful to have *Tread Loudly* be selected for the BrainTrust Ink imprint. I sincerely appreciate the opportunity to be part of this community of women who, together, are working to empower women in business and champion the equality of all people.

Lastly, to the young women to whom this book is dedicated, you are my inspiration and my teachers in life. Amanda Laabs, I am blown away by your intelligence, maturity, sense of self, wisdom, and ability to persevere. I'll always be your biggest fan. Amanda Mouradian-Koenig, you are the most thoughtful, compassionate, and ethical person I know. You make me want to be a better person. Emma Mae Santiago, you have so much love in your heart. You are the calm in every storm, an eternal optimist, and you sprinkle joy and laughter everywhere you go. Mae Santiago, although you're only a toddler, you bring a love to our family that is indescribable. Elizabeth Rybacki, from finishing college in three years, to nailing your first job, to your passion projects, I couldn't be prouder of you. You are a tiny package of huge ambition. Casey Larsen, the great lover of books and literature. I love watching you follow your passion to create a life that is authentically you. Sarah Kountz, you are the perfect balance of seriousness, fun, determination, free spirit, and inquisitiveness. Whatever you do in life, I know it will be filled with passion and meaning. Sophia Larsen, your smile and your energy light up every room you walk into. I can't wait to see what the future holds for you in college and beyond. Morgan Merbeth, the girl born to my best friend on my birthday. I admire your ability to take the things you are passionate about and create a life that is true to you. Kenzie Merbeth, you've handled the hardest parts of life with maturity and grace far beyond your years. I truly admire your strength, poise, and how you carry yourself in the world. Lindsey Neurauter, when you were a tiny girl your mom called you "little girl, BIG personality." It's a perfect description of the determined, confident, smart, and talented teenager you've become. I can't wait to see what the future holds for every one of you.

To my nephews, you are no less a part of my being and of this book than your sisters and cousins. You inspire me and touch my soul in so many ways. Alex Laabs, one of the most deeply feeling people I know. Your love, dedication, and compassion for family and your animals touches me more than I can put into words. You are the rock upon which your Buddah relies, and I'm so thankful for you. Thomas Kountz, you are the best brother that your sisters could have hoped for. You are the perfect example of what a hard-working, ethical, compassionate, considerate teenager can be. I can't wait to see what life holds for you in college and beyond. And Atlas, you are the ray of sunshine in our family.

Amanda, Amanda, Emma, Mae, Elizabeth, Casey, Sarah, Sophia, Morgan, Kenzie, Lindsey, Alex, Thomas, and Atlas: You are the reason I needed and wanted to write this book. You are my inspiration. When I feel disillusioned with the world, I remind myself that I need to continue the fight so the future will be a better place for you. You make me better. You make me want to do better. You have taught me so much, individually and collectively. And I love you with all my heart.

Notes

Introduction

1. For example, see National Association for Law Placement 2021 Report on Diversity in U.S. Law Firms, https://www.nalp.org/uploads/2021NALPReportonDiversity. pdf. See also, Ellen Milligan and Todd Gillespie, "Diversity at Elite Law Firms is So Bad Clients are Docking Fees," *Bloomberg*, October 5, 2021. https://www. bloomberg.com/news/articles/2021-10-05/big-law-has-a-diversity-problem-and-corporate-clients-are-stepping-in.

Chapter 3: If You Could Do Anything, What Would It Be?

1. For those who are not familiar with the hierarchy of university faculty, tenure-track law professors are those who teach substantive law classes and who are hired on a full-time, long-term basis. Law schools routinely employ other adjuncts and non-tenure-track professors, typically on a year-to-year and part-time basis, to teach legal writing and non-core courses. While still desirable, the non-tenure-track positions do not hold the same security of position, level of compensation, or prestige as the tenure-track positions. So, of course, I set my sights on the tenure-track positions.

2. No author, "Spring Self-Reported Entry-Level Hiring Report 2014," May 2014. https://prawfsblawg.blogs.com/prawfsblawg/2014/05/spring-self-reported-entry-level-hiring-report-2014.html.

3. "Spring Self-Reported Entry-Level Hiring Report 2014," May 2014. https:// prawfsblawg.blogs.com/prawfsblawg/2014/05/spring-self-reported-entry-level-hiring-report-2014.html.

4. For example, see Tara Sophia Mohr, "Why Women Don't Apply for Jobs Unless They Are 100% Qualified," *Harvard Business Review*, August 25, 2014. https://hbr. org/2014/08/why-women-dont-apply-for-jobs-unless-theyre-100-qualified/.

Chapter 4: There Is No Such Thing as "Having It All"

1. Eve Rodsky, *Fair Play: A Game-Changing Solution for When You Have Too Much to Do (and More Life to Live)* (New York: Penguin Random House, 2019). For more on this topic, see also Eve Rodsky, *Find Your Unicorn Space: Reclaim Your Creative Life in a Too-Busy World* (New York: G.P. Putnam's Sons, 2021).

2. Jennifer Siebel Newsom, dir., *Fair Play* (July 8, 2022; Los Angeles: Hello Sunshine).

Chapter 5: Representation Matters

1. McKinsey & Company, *McKinsey fact sheet*. https://www.mckinsey.com/~/media/McKinsey/About%20Us/Media%20Center/McKinsey-media-fact-sheet-Aug-2020.pdf.

2. Sheryl Sandberg, *Lean In: Women, Work, and the Will to Lead* (New York: Alfred A. Knopf, 2013).

3. See the mission statement of *Lean In* at https://leanin.org.

4. McKinsey & Company, "Women in the Workplace 2022," October 18, 2022. https://www.mckinsey.com/featured-insights/diversity-and-inclusion/women-in-the-workplace.

5. McKinsey & Company, "Women in the Workplace 2022," October 18, 2022, text preceding Exhibit 1. https://www.mckinsey.com/featured-insights/diversity-and-inclusion/women-in-the-workplace.

6. McKinsey & Company, "Women in the Workplace 2022," October 18, 2022, p. 54. https://www.mckinsey.com/featured-insights/diversity-and-inclusion/women-in-the-workplace/.

7. McKinsey & Company, "Women in the Workplace 2022," October 18, 2022, exhibit 1. https://www.mckinsey.com/featured-insights/diversity-and-inclusion/women-in-the-workplace.

8. McKinsey & Company, "Women in the Workplace 2022," Exhibit 1.

9. McKinsey & Company, "Women in the Workplace 2022," Exhibit 1.

10. McKinsey & Company, "Women in the Workplace 2022," Exhibit 1.

11. McKinsey & Company, "Women in the Workplace 2022," October 18, 2022, Exhibit 3. https://www.mckinsey.com/featured-insights/diversity-and-inclusion/women-in-the-workplace.

12. McKinsey & Company, "Women in the Workplace 2022," October 18, 2022. https://www.mckinsey.com/featured-insights/diversity-and-inclusion/women-in-the-workplace.

13. McKinsey & Company, "Women in the Workplace 2022."

14. McKinsey & Company, "Women in the Workplace 2022."

15. McKinsey & Company, "Women in the Workplace 2022."

16. McKinsey & Company, "Women in the Workplace 2022."

17. McKinsey & Company, "Women in the Workplace 2022," October 18, 2022, Exhibit 4. https://www.mckinsey.com/featured-insights/diversity-and-inclusion/women-in-the-workplace.

18. McKinsey & Company, "Women in the Workplace 2022."

Chapter 6: Don't Let Their Judgments Define You

1. Jennifer Aniston, "For the Record," *Huffington Post*, July 12, 2016. https://www.huffpost.com/entry/for-the-record_b_57855586e4b03fc3ee4e626f.

Chapter 7: Confronting Locker Room Talk

1. NBC News, "Donald Trump Makes Lewd Remarks About Women on Video," posted to YouTube October 7, 2016. https://www.youtube.com/watch?v=fYqKx1GuZGg.
2. National Public Radio, "Transcript: Michelle Obama's Speech on Donald Trump's Alleged Treatment of Women," NPR Politics web page, October 13, 2016. https://www.npr.org/2016/10/13/497846667/transcript-michelle-obamas-speech-on-donald-trumps-alleged-treatment-of-women.

Chapter 9: It Takes More Than Grit

1. Merriam-Webster Dictionary, "Grit." https://www.merriam-webster.com/dictionary/grit.
2. Angela Duckworth, "About Angela." https://angeladuckworth.com/about-angela/.
3. Angela Duckworth, "FAQs," https://angeladuckworth.com/qa/.
4. Angela Duckworth, "FAQs," https://angeladuckworth.com/qa/.
5. For purposes of maintaining the anonymity of the student and family discussed, I refrain from providing sources for the data regarding the school described herein.
6. For purposes of maintaining the anonymity of the student and family discussed, I refrain from providing sources for the data regarding the school described herein.
7. American Bar Association Commission on Women in the Profession, The American Bar Association. https://www.americanbar.org/groups/diversity/women/about_us/.
8. Commission on Women in the Profession, The American Bar Association.
9. ABA Commission on Women in the Profession: The Grit Project Program Toolkit Brochure, The American Bar Association. https://www.americanbar.org/content/dam/aba/administrative/women/grit_toolkit_brochure.pdf.
10. Martha Middleton, "ABA's Grit Project Aims to Help Women Advance in the Profession," *American Bar Association Journal*, November 1, 2014. https://www.abajournal.com/magazine/article/true_grit_a_new_aba_project_helps_women_learn_personal_characteristics_that.
11. The Grit Project, The American Bar Association. https://www.americanbar.org/groups/diversity/women/initiatives_awards/grit-project/.
12. The Grit Project, The American Bar Association.
13. The Grit Project, "21 Day Grit and Growth Mindset Project," The American Bar Association. https://www.americanbar.org/groups/diversity/women/initiatives_awards/grit-project/21-day-about/.

Chapter 10: Quitting Is Not Failure

1. Reese Witherspoon, "We Have to Change the Idea That a Woman With Ambition is Only Out for Herself," *Glamour,* September 5, 2017. https://www.glamour.com/story/reese-witherspoon-october-2017-cover-interview.

2. Adam McKay, dir., *Talladega Nights: The Ballad of Ricky Bobby* (2006; Culver City, CA: Sony Pictures Entertainment).

3. David Frankel, dir., *The Devil Wears Prada* (2006; Los Angeles: 20th Century Fox). Based on Lauren Weisberger, *The Devil Wears Prada* (New York: Broadway Books, 2003).

Chapter 11: Where Do We Go from Here?

1. Emma Watson, "HeForShe UN Speech," UN General Assembly, New York City, September 21, 2014, https://awpc.cattcenter.iastate.edu/2017/03/09/heforshe-u-n-speech-sept-21-2014/.

2. Emma Hinchliffe, "The Number of Women Running Fortune 500 Companies Reaches a Record High," *Fortune,* May 23, 2022. https://fortune.com/2022/05/23/female-ceos-fortune-500-2022-women-record-high-karen-lynch-sarah-nash/.

3. McKinsey & Company, "Women in the Workplace 2022," October 18, 2022. https://www.mckinsey.com/featured-insights/diversity-and-inclusion/women-in-the-workplace.

4. Gayle King, "Female Founders: Leading with Purpose," *O Quarterly* vol. 2 No. 3, 2022. https://www.magzter.com/stories/Lifestyle/The-Oprah-US/Female-Founders-Leading-With-Purpose. See also, U.S. Small Business Administration, "A Year of Historic Achievements for Women-owned Businesses," December 23, 2021. https://proxy.www.sba.gov/blog/year-historic-achievements-women-owned-businesses.

5. Female Founders Fund, "About Us." https://femalefoundersfund.com/about/.

6. Rebecca Leppert and Drew Desilver, "118th Congress Has a Record Number of Women," Pew Research Center, January 3, 2023. https://www.pewresearch.org/fact-tank/2023/01/03/118th-congress-has-a-record-number-of-women/.

7. United States Census Bureau, "Quick Facts: United States." https://www.census.gov/quickfacts/fact/table/US/LFE046220.

8. Simone Pathe, "Female Governors Will Break a Record in 2023," CNN, November 9, 2022. https://www.cnn.com/2022/11/09/politics/female-governors-record/index.html.

9. Liz Crampton, "There are Just 9 Female Governors. Both Parties Want Change," *Politico,* September 29, 2021. https://www.politico.com/news/2021/09/29/the-fifty-women-governors-499533.

10. Patrick Ryan, Maria Puente, and Carly Mallenbaum, "A Complete List of the 60 Bill Cosby Accusers and Their Reactions to His Prison Sentence," *USA Today,* April 27, 2018. https://www.usatoday.com/story/life/people/2018/04/27/bill-cosby-full-list-accusers/555144002/.

11. Charlie Savage, "Bill Cosby's Release from Prison, Explained," *New York Times,* July 1, 2021. https://www.nytimes.com/2021/07/01/arts/television/bill-cosby-conviction-overturned-why.html.

12. Michael E. Miller, "A Steep Price to Pay for 20 Minutes of Action: Dad Defends Stanford Sex Offender," *Washington Post*, June 6, 2016. https://www. washingtonpost.com/news/morning-mix/wp/2016/06/06/a-steep-price-to-pay-for-20-minutes-of-action-dad-defends-stanford-sex-offender/.

13. Emanuella Grinberg and Catherine E. Shoichet, "Brock Turner Released from Jail after Serving 3 Months for Sexual Assault," CNN, September 2, 2016. https://www. cnn.com/2016/09/02/us/brock-turner-release-jail/index.html.

14. Chanel Miller, *Know My Name: A Memoir* (New York: Penguin Books, 2019).

15. Kim Bellware, "Here Are the Women Publicly Accusing Roger Ailes of Sexual Harassment," *Huffington Post*, August 12, 2016. https://www.huffpost.com/entry/roger-ailes-accusers-list_n_57a9fa19e4b06e52746db865.

16. John Koblin, Emily Steel, and Jim Rutenberg, "Roger Ailes Leaves Fox News, and Rupert Murdoch Steps In," *New York Times*, July 21, 2016. https://www.nytimes.com/2016/07/22/business/media/roger-ailes-fox-news.html.

17. Olivia B. Waxman, "Ruth Bader Ginsburg Wishes this Case Had Legalized Abortion Instead of *Roe v. Wade*," *Time*, updated June 24, 2022; originally published August 2, 2018. https://time.com/5354490/ruth-bader-ginsburg-roe-v-wade/.

About the Author

Kristine Cherek is an attorney, former law professor, writer, and philanthropist. She began her career practicing real estate law at an international law firm. By age 33, she was the general counsel for one of the nation's largest real estate development companies. She currently serves on multiple nonprofit boards where she advocates for arts education, equity and access in higher education, and animal welfare. She is a 6-time marathon runner, former college cheerleader, and avid Marquette University alumni. She and her husband reside in Ponte Vedra Beach, Florida, with their two rescue cats.